# *A Shenandoah Promise*

## By Ariana Mangum

Righter Books

Copyright 2012 by Ariana Mangum
All rights reserved

No part of this may be reproduced in any form without permission of the author and publisher.

Righter Publishing Company, Inc.
410 River Oaks Parkway
Timberlake, North Carolina 27583

Cover by Barbara Alston

www.righterbooks.com

January 2014
Second Version 2015

Printed and bound in the United States of America

Library of Congress Control Number
2014930424

ISBN: 978-1-938527-22-7
A Shenandoah Promise
By Ariana Mangum

Available on Amazon Kindle

O, Shenandoah, I long to hear you
Away, you rolling river
O, Shenandoah, I long to see you
Away, we're bound away
'Cross the wide Missouri

—traditional American folk
song and sea shanty

**Dedication**

This book is dedicated to my granddaughter, Celia Perry, who also made a transoceanic voyage as a small child to begin a new life in America.

# *A Shenandoah Promise*

## A BIG DECISION

When Robert Jones was injured after he fell in an unused mineshaft in Abergavenny, South Wales, he decided to accept a land grant in North Frederick County, near Winchester, Virginia.

"I can't go down in the mines again," he told his wife Sarah. "And there's a good hundred acres being offered in Virginia. We can go to America and start anew with a farm."

"You don't know anything about farming," Sarah insisted. "I like the life here in the Welsh valleys. Mining is all you know. You've been down in the mines all your life."

Sarah, a small, shy woman, could speak some English but felt much more comfortable speaking Welsh. She did not wish to leave her native land and travel to America, a country filled with uncivilized natives, French trappers, and wild Indians.

In spite of her protestations and his lack of farming experience, Robert decided they would leave their home in the Welsh valleys and seek a new life in Virginia's Shenandoah Valley. Their two daughters, Annie and Ellen, both in their twenties, would accompany their parents to America.

Secretly, Annie packed Granny Jones's teapot in her carpetbag amongst her clothes. It was the only reminder of their old life that she could bring with her. It always made a wonderful cup of tea, and Ellen was sure it would be useful in their new home.

In May of 1828, after the family sold most of its possessions, Robert took his wife and daughters to Cardiff, Wales's capital city. He needed to get emigration papers for his family and inquire about sailing ships leaving for Philadelphia from Bristol on the River Avon.

Robert's cousin Hugh Jones often traveled to Cardiff to deliver goods. He also made trips to Bristol for his deliveries. Hugh had friends and relatives in Cardiff and in Bristol with whom the family could stay overnight during the journey.

After they obtained their emigration papers in Cardiff, the family traveled for two days and nights until they reached the English port of Bristol. The ship that was to take them to America was *The West Wind*. It was a new steamship, with sails to supplement the steam power, and it was much faster than older ships. On the evening tide, *The West Wind* spread her sails, and with Robert Jones and his family aboard, the ship left Bristol for Philadelphia.

It all happened so fast that Sarah had little time to protest. Although they looked forward to being on dry land, Ellen and Annie viewed the long trip across the ocean as the first step in a new adventure. Their mother, however, found the voyage very difficult. With the ship's constant motion and her increasing distance from home, Sarah felt both seasick and homesick.

"I'm not staying with a lot of savages in the wilderness," she told her husband, as she lay on her bunk feeling lost and afraid. The Joneses' tiny space was not made to house four people, and the family did its best despite the crowded and cramped accommodations. Sarah was frequently cross or ill, and she demanded privacy. Robert tended to her needs while their daughters went for long walks on the ship's deck.

"I'm not going to like Winchester one bit," Sarah insisted. "You can't farm a hundred acres all by yourself, and don't expect to make workhorses out of Ellen and Annie."

The family landed in America in the middle of June, and they found the city of Philadelphia hot and humid.

"Look!" Annie cried with delight. "It's a big city with real houses, churches, shops, and Europeans. There are no Indians, Mother. Just look at it."

Robert escorted his family down the docks toward a large office. Here, he got information about where they could stay in the city and when the next wagon train might leave to go across southeastern Pennsylvania and travel down as far as Virginia's Shenandoah Valley.

Robert learned that Winchester was at the northern end of the valley. Thomas Wood, who had emigrated from Winchester, England, founded it in 1741. Winchester, Virginia, was a sizeable town of 9,000 residents and 288 slaves.

Winchester was the fourth city in Virginia to receive a charter. George Washington had spent several years there surveying Lord Fairfax's land grant of many thousands of acres. It was part of the old Shawnee campgrounds before the tribe crossed the Allegheny Mountains into the Ohio River Valley.

From Philadelphia, the immigrants had to cross the Great Valley, part of Valley Forge, where Washington spent a cold winter with his troops during the Revolutionary War. They followed the old Indian Path, later called the Great Wagon Road after a treaty in 1744 with the Indians that allowed the colonists to use the route. It was a safe road through southeastern Pennsylvania, Maryland, and Virginia. For over a century, many wagon trains, each made up of about sixteen wagons, rattled down this great route into the Shenandoah Valley and the Carolinas.

Since Virginia's Governor Gooch was tolerant in his policies, Frederick County and Winchester welcomed Scots Presbyterians, English Quakers, English Anglicans, and German Lutherans. It was an old and friendly town. When he learned this, Robert Jones felt sure that he, a Welshman and a Methodist, would also be welcomed.

"Mrs. Wilkinson has a well-run boarding house on Locust Street," the official behind the desk reassured Robert. "There are wagons waiting outside to transport passengers from the docks to wherever they're staying. You will also want to contact the Great Wagon Road office, which is not far from here."

Clutching the paper with Mrs. Wilkinson's address, Robert escorted his family across the street, where he found several wagons waiting, each drawn by two stout horses. Robert asked the first driver in line to take them to Locust Street. The driver helped Sarah onto her seat and placed the family's bundles in the wagon bed.

As the wagon moved forward, the travelers looked in awe at their surroundings. Philadelphia, a port city, was full of commerce, and there were throngs of people coming and going. The driver continued up Spruce Street and turned onto Jessop. After a short distance, they reached Locust Street, lined with neat red brick houses built close to the pavement. Halfway down, the driver brought his horses to a halt in front of Mrs. Wilkinson's boarding house. He helped Sarah down from the wagon and handed the girls and Robert their bundles.

Robert still had English money and was not sure of the amount he should pay, but the driver was trustworthy and charged him an honest fare. The family thanked the driver, and Robert walked up to the entrance and hit the brass knocker.

A young girl opened the door. She was about twenty, with a curious, pleasant face and light brown hair.

"Yes, sir, what is it?" she asked.

"I understand you let rooms," Robert said. "We were hoping to find some place to stay until we could make arrangements to go to Virginia."

"We do let rooms," the servant girl replied. She stood aside to allow the tired family to pass into the hallway.

"Mrs. Wilkinson will be right down. Come into the parlor," she said, pushing the door ajar and leading them into a neatly furnished room. "Please, have a seat."

A few minutes later the owner, Mrs. Wilkinson, appeared. She quickly looked over her visitors and, seeing that they were neatly dressed, she asked only a few questions. She noted that Mr. Jones was well-spoken although he had an accent, and she readily offered the family accommodation.

"I don't know how long we'll stay. We plan to take the wagon train to Winchester, Virginia, as soon as I can arrange it," Robert explained. "We've come from Wales. My wife speaks only a little English."

Mrs. Wilkinson saw that Sarah appeared very tired. "I'll show you the room. It's nice and quiet and has good windows. But first, may I get you something cool to drink?"

Sarah shook her head although she felt worn out after the long sea journey and the drive to Locust Street in the heat.

Mrs. Wilkinson sent Maggie, the young girl, to get them some cold water. Meanwhile, Annie unpacked her Granny's teapot and shyly asked Mrs. Wilkinson, "Could you please make my mother a cup of tea in this teapot? I'm sure it will help her to feel better."

She explained that she had brought the teapot with her from Wales because it always made a grand cup of tea.

"It's wonderful," Mrs. Wilkinson declared. "I've never seen anything like it!" The teapot was decorated with a nautical scene and a picture of a Welsh chorus.

"Yes, it's very special and has been in our family a long time," Ellen explained. "But I'm not sure if we have any tea left."

"Oh, I have some," Mrs. Wilkinson replied. She handed the teapot to Maggie. "Guard this with your life," she warned. "It's very special. Go and set the water to boil and make Mrs. Jones a cup of strong English brewed tea."

Maggie held the teapot as if it were a precious jewel. Then she left the room and returned a few minutes later with a tray on which were five cups, sugar, and milk.

The magic teapot sat in the middle with steam rising from its spout. Carefully, Maggie poured the hot liquid into a cup and passed it to Sarah along with a spoon and saucer. Then she offered a plate of little cakes and bread with jam.

"Thank you," said a grateful Sarah. "Thank you."

"Mrs. Wilkinson, would you like to pour the tea while I get more cakes from the kitchen?" Maggie asked.

"No, Maggie, you finish what you're doing," Mrs. Wilkinson said. "I'll get the other cakes."

Maggie spread a napkin on Sarah's lap and then offered each guest a cup of tea from the magic teapot. Mrs. Wilkinson reappeared with extra cakes and passed them to the family.

"Ah," said Annie, sipping her tea. "I told you that Granny Jones's teapot was magic."

"Yes, indeed," replied Mrs. Wilkinson. "I've never tasted such a good cup of tea. Surely it must be magic."

After the family finished eating, Maggie showed them a spacious room overlooking the back garden. Sarah lay down on the bed and almost immediately fell asleep.

Robert left in search of the booking office for the wagon trains, which traveled to the Shenandoah Valley on a weekly basis in the summer. He learned that the wagons were almost fully booked for the next week, but he was able to secure places for himself and his family on one of the Conestoga wagons for the following Monday.

"Be here early," the agent warned him. "We depart with sixteen wagons at nine o'clock. You will be in wagon number two with John Row's team. We leave early because we have to cross the Conestoga River, and we want to do that before it gets dark." The Jones family were about to follow the historic route of many immigrants before them from the British Isles and the Palatinate region of Germany.

"William Penn's city is very interesting," Mrs. Wilkinson told Robert. "Maybe you and your girls would like to explore it. Philadelphia is very modern, with paved avenues and street lighting. There are many public buildings, which are interesting, especially Independence Hall, where the early patriots held the Continental Congress. You can also see the Liberty Bell, which is cracked. It cracked when it was first rung to declare America's independence from England."

"We must go and visit Independence Hall, and I'd like to see the Liberty Bell, too," Annie told her father.

"Yes, you should," Mrs. Wilkinson agreed. "Philadelphia is like a European city. It's laid out with wide avenues, and the unique red-brick houses were built in the last century. It also has the first lending library in America, thanks to Benjamin Franklin. The Philadelphia Academy for Art, founded by Charles Willson Peale, was the first one in America."

"It sounds like a very interesting place," Ellen said, eager to explore their new world.

"It certainly is!" agreed Mrs. Wilkinson. She knew the history of her city well and felt proud of its accomplishments. "Mr. Franklin gathered around him several learned men," she continued. "Among them were John Bartram, the botanist, and the physician John Morgan. Mr. Franklin also brought to Philadelphia Ebenezer Kinnersley, who investigated the source of electricity, as did Franklin himself. Philadelphia is known not only for famous men of science, but also for artists and writers. It also had the first Academy for Arts and Sciences in America."

"Could you draw a map for us?" Robert asked his hostess. "We look forward to exploring your beautiful city."

"I can easily do that, Mr. Jones. I shall give you

directions to Carpenter's Hall, where the first Continental Congress met to draw up a list of grievances against the mother country. This brought the colonies into rebellion with England, which led to the war for our independence. Philadelphia had a difficult time when the British occupied the city that terribly cold winter of 1777-1778. For several weeks, Washington and his troops lived in huts at Valley Forge just west of the city. Oh, but I'm getting carried away! I mustn't forget to draw you a map." Mrs. Wilkinson left the room to make one for the family.

Robert took Annie and Ellen to see the sights of William Penn's and Benjamin Franklin's famous city. They explored Independence Hall, and even went down to Arch Street to see the exterior of Betsy Ross's house.

"She's the woman who designed the first American flag," Robert explained. "With a snip of her scissors, she cut a white six-point star. Then she made thirteen of them for the thirteen original colonies. She sewed these stars onto a field of blue. After that, she made the red and white stripes." Mrs. Wilkinson had told Robert about Betsy Ross, and he wondered how she was able to make a six-point star with only a snip of her scissors.

After their long walk exploring the city, Robert and his girls stopped in a park to rest their feet. They bought pretzels from a pushcart and fed the birds with the crumbs.

"I must tell Mrs. Wilkinson how much we've enjoyed exploring Philadelphia," Annie said.

"I like feeding the birds, too," said Ellen. "I also like American food."

"Yes," agreed Robert. "The pretzels are very good. The man from the pushcart told me that they were introduced by the Dutch in colonial times."

Three days later, Robert and his family said farewell to Mrs. Wilkinson and walked through Philadelphia's historic streets until they came to the booking office. Here, as planned, a team of horses waited, hitched to a large wagon. It would take them out of the city to the Great Valley and on to Yellow Springs Road. This road would bring them to the staging ground for the wagon train to the Shenandoah Valley.

The first Conestoga wagons to make the trek into the valley had been built by German blacksmiths. It was a feat in building, because the wagons were designed in the shape of a boat and the wheels could be removed to make a vessel suitable for crossing rivers. These wagons were constructed for long trips and had been named for the Conestoga River, which ran through Lancaster County, Pennsylvania.

Later, the wagons were introduced into North Carolina and other areas where the German immigrants settled. This type of wagon became the prairie schooner of the Western territories and was usually pulled by a team of four or six horses.

## THE JOURNEY TOWARD WINCHESTER

Most of the wagon teams left the city in the late summer, after harvest time. The trip to the Shenandoah Valley took the settlers three weeks. The wagons were heavily loaded with household goods and food from the harvest. These wagons could carry ten tons. Earlier trips made up of mostly Scots, Scots-Irish, Germans, and Pennsylvania Dutch had as their destinations the Lower Valley places like Winchester, Strasburg, and New Town. These wagons were not as full because the trip was shorter. After their long sea journey from England, this shorter trip suited Robert much better.

"I'm sorry to say farewell to Philadelphia," Annie told her father. "It's quite a good-size city."

"I'm also sorry to leave," Robert agreed, as they approached the man who would take them to meet the wagon train. "Are you Samuel Hicks?" he asked.

"Yes, I am," the driver replied. "Are you Mr. Jones, Mr. Robert Jones? I am to take you and your family out to the Great Valley, where you'll join the wagon train to go west."

Robert acknowledged who he and his family were. Sarah, still half-asleep, allowed Samuel to help her. She felt cross and tired, and she certainly did not wish to bounce around in an open wagon for several hours. However, she managed to say "good morning" in English and "thank you" when the teamster settled her and their bundles into the wagon in preparation for their journey.

"How far is it to the Great Valley?" Robert asked. "Where do we meet the wagon train?"

"It's not far," Samuel replied. "We follow Valley Creek out for a while, and then we turn off onto Yellow Springs Road."

Once settled in the wagon, the family waited for Samuel to cluck to his horses and drive them out of the city. Quickly, the polite young man packed away the horses' feedbags and their wooden buckets for water. Then he mounted the wagon, sat down on the hard wooden seat, and picked up the reins. The big team of brown draft horses pushed forward into their collars, and the family was on its way to join the wagon train.

The team moved into Philadelphia's morning traffic of vendors' carts, commercial wagons, and the carriages of businessmen. The sun rose and promised a hot day. As they left the city and headed toward the Great Valley, the woods and open ground allowed a breeze to blow down the road beside Valley Creek. By noon, the little party joined several Conestoga wagons waiting for other immigrants to gather.

"Here we are," said Samuel. He pulled his team to a halt. "This is where the wagons assemble to go west."

"I'll jump down and find the foreman," Robert said.

"Go over to that shed on the right," Samuel directed. "You'll find Mr. James Harrison inside and he'll tell you which wagon is yours. He's with a man called Hans Krumper, a German from Lancaster County; he helps the German-speaking clients."

Robert did as Samuel suggested and entered the shed. Inside he found both Hans Krumper and Mr. Harrison.

"Good morning," Robert greeted them. "I've come to join your wagon train. My name is Robert Jones—my family and I should be on your list of travelers."

"Let me consult my list," said Mr. Harrison as he scanned the names on a long sheet of paper. "Ah, yes. Your name is down here, and also your wife's and two girls'."

"That's right. We've just come from Philadelphia this morning. I think we're assigned to wagon number two."

"That's Charlie's wagon. He's already here. That's his team tethered down by the creek over to the left. Just ask for Charlie Smithson. He has copper-red hair—you can't miss him. He has a team of four big draft horses almost the same color as his hair. You'll have no trouble finding him."

Down by the creek, Robert found four chestnut horses being watered and fed by a man with red hair. As Robert approached, he asked, "Are you Charlie?"

"Yes, I'm Charlie, and this is my team. Grand horses they are, too. Full of the Old Nick and strong work animals. You must be Robert Jones. I'm pleased to meet you." Charlie offered him a wet hand.

Robert watched the country man hitch his team to a Conestoga wagon. The draft horses appeared docile and patient. After he hooked up the traces to the singletrees on the wagon and settled the four horses, Charlie told Robert to collect his family.

"We'll join the wagons in half an hour," Charlie said. He explained that John Row, to whose team Robert and his family were first assigned, was not on the wagon train. "One of his horses threw a shoe and is lame. So I came instead. We'll soon be off," he reminded Robert, "so be on time."

"I'll be back shortly," Robert promised, and he went to find his wife and girls.

About five hundred yards away, a crowd had gathered around a campfire. Here, Annie boiled water and served her mother and sister each a cup of tea. Then she offered some to the other travelers.

"It's very good tea," she explained as she filled their cups.

Several immigrants found more cups and offered sugar to their fellow travelers. While Annie was thus engaged, Robert arrived. "Come on, we must get ready to leave," he said.

"Surely, you'll have some tea, Father," suggested Ellen, as she poured out the remaining water.

Robert knew it would be rude to break up the party,

so he accepted a cup. "Now, we must get ready to leave," he told them. "You see that team of chestnut horses over there by the creek? That's Charlie's team and his wagon. We're going with him. Close up your bag, Annie, and I'll douse the fire."

Robert took a bucket and went to the creek for some water. After thanking Annie and Ellen for the tea party, the crowd left and went to find their wagons. Slowly, the wagon train formed. Robert found Sarah among four other Welsh women.

"Come on," Robert told her. "We must get ready to go."

"Did you hear what the women were saying?" Sarah asked excitedly. "They speak Welsh! They are also going to Winchester. They tell me there are people in the town who are Welsh-speaking and who are Methodists."

While they loaded up the wagon, Charlie chatted with Robert. "You see that man over beside that clump of trees with a cigar in his mouth? That cigar is called a 'stogie' after the Conestoga wagons because the tobacco that wraps the cigar is grown in Lancaster County. You'll see a lot of the teamsters smoking stogies."

Charlie guided his four horses onto the Lancaster Pike, which would take them through the rolling countryside interspersed with neat homesteads and maturing fields of corn and wheat.

"What are your horses' names?" Annie asked as she climbed up front onto the seat beside Charlie, eager to see where they were headed. Ellen sat on the other side while their father and mother rode in the back of the wagon. Charlie commanded his team to "walk on."

"Are these horses really well-behaved? They are so very big," Ellen said, feeling uneasy.

Charlie laughed. "I call them Washington, Adams, Jefferson, and Madison after the presidents. Most people call their horses by short names, but I feel these names are grand for such lovely large animals. Don't you agree?"

"They're noble-looking creatures and should have noble names," Annie replied. "These names fit your beautiful horses. We're riding with the presidents, so we should get to Winchester safely."

"You have to watch Madison," Charlie said. "He's young and a bit flighty. He doesn't like barking dogs and jumps away from them. Now, Washington and Adams, the two-wheelers, are older and more steady. Jefferson is the ruddiest of the team, and he has a temper just like his namesake. He and Madison are the leaders because they are lighter and faster, but not as steady and dependable as Washington and Adams, who pull the wagon the hardest and carry the heaviest load. The leaders help, but they're not the workers that the wheelers are. Washington and Adams are very reliable."

"How long does this good road last?" Ellen wanted to know. "Isn't this a city road?"

"Yes, this is Lancaster Pike, and it's maintained for a good ways, but once we get through Lancaster County, the road becomes dirt and gravel," Charlie told her. "The German families, called 'Pennsylvania Dutch,' keep the roads in good repair so they can bring their vegetables and meats to the markets in Philadelphia and to the farmers' markets in Lancaster. They're a thrifty people, and their farms are always neat and productive. Once we go over the Susquehanna River, the road becomes rougher."

"Do the Pennsylvania Dutch speak English?" Annie asked, interested in the neat farms and the barns decorated with stars and colorful hex signs.

"Some of them speak very good English. They have to, in order to sell produce and baked goods to travelers from their farms. You can buy some tasty foods when we get into Mennonite country. Mennonites are a very conservative group of German Protestants. The women set up long tables at the roadside and sell wonderful shoo-fly pies and pickled relish and German breads. Oh yes, we shall eat well through Lancaster County." Charlie laughed with pleasure at the thought of the good food to come. "We have great times until we come to the Susquehanna River. Shortly after Gettysburg, the road becomes rough and the mountains begin."

"Where will we spend the night?" Ellen asked. "I don't fancy living open to the rain and the bugs. How do we wash and cook our meals?"

"We'll sleep in the wagon. At Coatesville, there's a stream for water, and the wagons can stay in the ferryman's pasture. There are stones placed to make fireplaces. The only problem at Wright's Ferry on the Susquehanna is that the wagons take a long time to cross. The river is deep and swift and can cause trouble. Sometimes all the wagons don't make it over before dark, and so they have to finish crossing in the morning."

Annie and Ellen continued to question Charlie about their journey through Pennsylvania.

"When do we stop for lunch?" Annie felt hungry. "I brought my Granny's teapot with me, and I can make you a good cup of tea."

"We'll stop soon. We like to camp at Valley Creek. Then we'll have a long drive until sundown. Coatesville is about thirty-five miles from there and really farther than we need to go. But with the hard gravel road and the good footing, we try to keep on that schedule. On good roads, we can cover twenty-five miles a day. When we get closer to the mountains, we can only make fifteen miles a day. The roads are not as well maintained and the land is rocky," Charlie explained as they drove toward their campground.

At noon, the caravan stopped beside a fast-flowing creek. Ed, the wagon master, called to the teamsters to "pull over into that big pasture and we'll halt for lunch."

Charlie pulled the wagon off the road, and Robert jumped out of the back of the wagon and came to hold the leaders as Charlie helped the women to gather their picnic hampers. "I'll take the horses down to the creek for a drink," Robert offered. "Then they can graze over across the field away from the crowd."

Robert unhitched Jefferson and Madison and led them toward the creek. The horses drank thirstily, and Madison pawed at the fast-flowing cold water. Jefferson drizzled water from his mouth and watched the other horses gather in the pasture. Blankets were spread on the ground. Sarah appeared and sat beside Charlie.

"Where are we?" she asked in English. "How far have we come since Philadelphia?"

"This is almost the end of Valley Creek. We'll stop here for an hour and eat our lunch. Ellen, jump down and fill this wooden bucket with water," Charlie directed, as he pulled out an iron cooking pot for her to use for the tea. Then he led the two-wheelers to drink in the swift-flowing stream. Adams pawed the water, but Washington drank eagerly. Charlie tied the horses so they could graze, and then he found a cooking pit in which to build a fire. Nearby, children played. They skipped rope and threw flat stones across the water.

"This is a terribly long trip," Sarah complained. "It's much too far to Virginia."

"Come on," Robert told her. "The girls have got a good lunch ready for you and a cup of tea."

"How long must we drive in this contraption? I'm hot and uncomfortable," Sarah complained in Welsh. "I knew we should have never come to America."

Soon their pot was boiling for tea and Ellen and Annie opened their hampers and laid out a tasty lunch under shade trees not far from the stream. Annie and Ellen found a smooth stump and laid out their meal on it. Charlie made the horses secure and then he helped Sarah over the rough ground to the picnic table.

"You'll get so you like this country," Charlie told

Sarah. "It's very civilized in the Pennsylvania German portion of Lancaster County. It has beautiful farms with rich wheat, corn, and flax fields. Virginia is very diverse, with Winchester its fourth city to receive a charter. It's pretty country, and near the mountains, not unlike Wales," he assured her.

"Robert knows nothing about farming. He knows only mines and coal. How will he manage with his bad legs?" Sarah asked. "Oh, there are certainly a lot of strange insects in America who want to share my lunch. Go away, shoo!"

"Robert can learn how to farm," Charlie replied. "All of these people on the wagon train will settle in the Shenandoah Valley, and they will make a good living. You'll like it once you're settled in your new home. It's the getting there that's difficult."

Charlie found a log, which he rolled up to their stump table and offered Sarah a seat. Then he sat down himself. Robert settled on Sarah's other side. Ellen and Annie served their cold meal and offered their mother some hot tea from Granny's teapot.

Hoping for a few leftover crumbs, birds chirped in the trees around them. A black bird chased away a family of robins, as he hoped to be the first at the birds' picnic. The horses, now free of their harness and tied with loose halters, grazed in contentment. They had extra mileage to go today, and Charlie liked to have his team as relaxed as possible. He gave them their oats and returned to the picnic table.

Other teamsters pulled their teams off the road, but not near enough to disturb Charlie's horses. There were wagons parked on both sides of the road while the drivers watered and fed animals. Children played by the roadside while their families climbed down from the wagons to prepare the noonday meal. Above them in the trees, the ever-vigilant crows called to each other to spread the news of an impending feast.

Charlie explained, "My father was a blacksmith, and he and several of his friends helped to build the Conestoga wagons. I don't usually come on these cross-country trips. Just sometimes when Ed needs an extra team, and I'm free. Usually, I farm and work at the blacksmith's forge in New Town. There are about six of us who work there. I'm a Scot from the Borders of England, Tweedside, and we like tinkering and making things. My father came to Virginia before I was born, so I am an American by birth."

"How far is it to Winchester?" Robert asked him.

"It's two hundred miles, more or less. It takes about three weeks if the rivers are not in spate and the weather is good. Sometimes it takes longer, but usually three weeks."

"Oh, dear, three weeks! I had no idea," said Robert, surprised by the distances in America.

"Where do we spend the night?" Annie inquired. "Are there any Indians?"

"Not anymore," Charlie assured her. "They've gone into the Ohio River Valley. The Shawnees, that is. There are a few Indians near the Alleghany Mountains. They don't bother us. The Germans from Lancaster County cleared the Indians out when they signed the treaty for the Great Wagon Road. The Indians went west, and others have come north, but they are also further west, closer to the Ohio River Valley. It's a hard way to travel, with the Susquehanna and the Potomac rivers to navigate. The German Palatines settled this country, and its great farmland. That's why so many people come this way to go into the Shenandoah Valley."

"Drivers up," shouted Ed Morrison, the wagon master. "Get your teams ready!"

The family packed the remains of their meal in hampers. Charlie helped Sarah and the two girls onto the high Conestoga wagon. He made the wooden seat more comfortable by placing blankets and a few cushions for

Sarah and her daughters. Then, as if by a magic signal, the teams prepared to leave. Fifteen minutes later, Ed called, "Everyone ready? Forward ho!"

The sixteen teams lined up and, without a lot of fuss, they moved off down Yellow Springs Road, which joined the Great Wagon Road. The teamsters drove their horses forward. The horses knew the drill and waited patiently for the wagon in front of them to take its place. Ed called out sixteen names. Each teamster replied, "Here," and slowly, the sixteen teams moved down the road. For the next half hour, the teamsters did not speak as the horses moved southwest along the road at a fast walk. Annie watched the whole process in awe. Within thirty minutes, the wagons passed over Valley Creek and gained the main road that would take them across southern Pennsylvania and down into Virginia.

Even Sarah was fascinated by the arrangement of the wagons as the teamsters drove them forward. Four draft horses pulled most wagons, and their drivers appeared to be especially skillful at handling them. The crows and robins watched them go, eager to enjoy the banquet, which awaited them. The birds sent messages to each other, and whole flocks descended on the pasture.

The wagon train continued through rolling farmland and headed southwest toward the Susquehanna, a major river that fed into the Chesapeake Bay.

"There are a few smaller streams," Charlie explained, "but the Susquehanna and later the Potomac are the really big rivers we must cross. You'll be surprised to know the wagon becomes a boat. We just take the wheels off, and because the front and back are higher than usual, the wagons can become a steady ship for navigating rivers."

"That's very clever," remarked Robert. "Who thought that up?"

"The Germans from Lancaster County," Charlie

explained. "They are clever people. They're ready for anything."

"You mean this wagon can become a boat? That's marvelous. Do you have paddles to take the boat across rivers?" Annie wanted to know.

"Yes, they are stored in the back. There are about six paddles. We can row the boat or we can pole it along. Usually we row it," Charlie explained. "We are ready for all kinds of rivers, from little ones to big ones like the Susquehanna and the Potomac. We can unhitch the horses and let them swim, or we can leave them hitched to the wagons if the stream is not too wide and swift. Sometimes the horses are better off swimming on their own with one of the teamsters. It depends upon the currents."

As the afternoon progressed toward evening, Charlie said, "We must put straps of bells on the horses. When it's dark, other teams can hear the bells and know there is traffic on the road. When we let the horses graze at night, we can find them by the sound of the bells. We also need two lanterns in front and another two on the back of the wagon."

Robert put bells on Madison while Charlie buckled a set each on Adams and Washington.

"Do you have an extra set?" a voice asked on the darkened road.

A young man appeared beside the wagon and looked up at Charlie on his high seat next to Annie and Ellen.

"There's a strap of bells I use on Jefferson, but he hates bells and dances all the time they are on him. You can use them if you like," Charlie offered.

"Yes, thank you, I need them for my leader. I lost my bells when their buckle broke," the young man explained. "I drive the team in front of yours with my father. My name is Johnny."

"You are welcome to use Jefferson's bells." Charlie

handed them to the young lad. "Do you have your lanterns as well?"

"Oh, yes, my grandfather has attended to the lights. Those are fine chestnut draft horses you have pulling your wagon. Our horses are too small for the heavy Conestoga, even if it's only half loaded."

Johnny put the bells on his leader and disappeared around the other side of the wagon. As the evening deepened, the tree toads and the cicadas sang their night music. An owl hooted in the woods, and the farm dogs barked. Then, all became silent.

## Typical buildings along their route

Cabin like Robert's

Typical I House in the Shenandoah Valley

German house door is off center

German barn with hex signs. Hex in German means *witch*.
The signs keep off the witches and bad spirits.

# MONTY

As the wagon train made its way down Lancaster Pike toward the Susquehanna River, a nondescript brown hound dog followed. At first, Charlie thought the dog belonged to one of the teamsters, or perhaps to one of the families in another wagon. The dog seemed to like Charlie and walked beside Adams just in front of the wagon wheel on the left-hand side.

"Is that your dog?" Ellen asked Johnny, who drove the team just ahead of Charlie's team.

"No, I've never seen him before. Could he belong to one of the farmers?"

"If he were a shepherd or a collie for herding cattle or sheep, he might belong to one of the German farmers. But that's a sporting dog, the kind we have in the South," Charlie remarked. "He looks like a pretty good one, not just a cur."

Annie named the dog 'Monty,' gave him some leftover food, and filled a small pan of water for him. "Now," she told the brown hound, "you are coming with us."

Ed, the wagon master, discouraged the travelers from bringing any pets along and chased away every stray dog. Annie found an old belt that one of the men had discarded and cut it down to the right size for a collar. Then she put it on Monty and tied a horse lead to it whenever Ed came around to check on the lead teams. Annie hid Monty in the woods and pretended she was washing dishes at the stream or was packing up her picnic hamper. No one else saw the brown hound, and no one objected.

"Whose dog is that?" asked Charlie on the third day after Monty joined them. "He's got a collar on, so he must belong to someone."

"Yes," Annie agreed. "He's a real pet, and he likes you, Charlie."

Monty took up his post just in front of the left wheel and trotted along contentedly beside Adams. The horse didn't seem to mind, and the wagon rode easily with the four horses pulling it and with Monty keeping guard.

Charlie had his suspicions about whether the dog was a stray when he saw Ellen slip him some food, but Charlie liked the brown hound and said nothing. A dog is a friendly animal, and in the country, most people had hunting dogs in the South. Charlie felt the Welsh family needed a companion in America, where everything was foreign to them.

"Do you know anything about this dog that has taken up with us?" Charlie asked Robert.

"No, he came a few days ago and just trots beside the left wheel of the wagon as if he belongs to us. I've never seen him before Monday and know nothing about him."

Charlie knew the family hadn't brought the dog with them, but a dog might cheer Robert's wife and give her a new interest for living in America.

"Annie, do you know anything about this stray dog?" Charlie asked her when they stopped for a rest. "Where did he come from, and where did he get the collar?"

Annie didn't reply because she feared Charlie might object and report her to Ed, the wagon master.

"He's coming with us," Ellen firmly announced. "Monty will protect us from wild animals. Annie's nursed his cut foot, and they're friends."

"Did you not hear the wagon master say there are no pets?" Charlie asked her.

"He's not the wagon master's responsibility," Annie said defiantly. "He's good and gentle, and he'll guard us and the horses, too. Anyway, I put the collar on him, and he's my dog now."

Charlie said no more. He left the dog with Ellen and

Annie and returned to his horses. Monty trotted beside Adams as if he owned them all. Annie sat down next to Charlie on the hard front seat. Ellen changed the subject.

Monty knew his job. He kept the road clear of stray farm animals and chased the white-tailed deer back into the forest. He guarded the wagon and its horses from fallen branches and other road hazards. Charlie smiled as he watched the dog trot beside the wagon. He liked a hound dog and felt that they made great family pets. Charlie respected Monty because he was sensible and knew his business. Yet, he knew the dog's presence might cause trouble with Ed, and he took care to keep Monty a secret.

The Conestoga River wound through Lancaster County. There was a new covered bridge over the river. Many of the horses were spooked by the hollow sound the wooden planking made under their hooves, so some of the horses and wagons splashed through the ford. It was not deep, and the horses easily walked across the river. Monty stopped to drink and swam part of the way to cool himself off. At the far side, the teams joined up again and took their places in line.

On the western side of the Conestoga River, amid fields of ripening corn, was a pasture surrounded by a board fence that belonged to a German farmer and his wife. Several pigs lived in the pasture, mostly red Duroc shoats. As the big horses and wagons followed one after another, the pigs felt threatened by all of the noise and commotion. The shoats squealed, and their screams sounded almost human as they scampered up the field.

One young pig broke loose from the rest and rolled under the board fence. He wriggled free just as Jefferson and Madison took their places in the wagon train.

Jefferson snorted and jumped to one side as the pig, now terrified, scrambled between the horses' hooves. Madison stood up on his hind legs, and the pig ran back toward the wheelers in an effort to get away.

Robert jumped down from the wagon and grabbed Jefferson's bridle in an attempt to hold him. "Whoa, whoa," he cried.

Charlie handed the reins to Annie and jumped down off the wagon. "Steady, boys. Steady," he said to Washington and Adams as he caught Adams by the bridle.

The frightened pig fled down the road with Monty at his heels. Charlie ran after them. Johnny heard the squealing from his wagon and handed the reins to his grandfather, then jumped down to help. Charlie and Johnny, working together, approached the pig from both sides and tried to grab a hind leg. Charlie finally caught hold of the pig's leg and, with Johnny's help, they lifted the pig out of the road. By this time, the farmer and his wife heard the commotion and came running across the pasture. The farmer opened the gate while his wife rushed to find a branch to block the hole in the fence. Charlie and Johnny held onto the squealing, wriggling animal as Monty danced around, barking with great excitement. Finally, the pig was returned to its owners.

Annie and Ellen watched in gales of laughter. "I'm sure that pig felt that all the witches in Lancaster County were chasing him," Annie said. Tears covered Ellen's face from so much merriment.

Monty watched the pig go, and then with his tail held high, the clever dog returned to his place beside Adams, as if to remark, "I've done my duty for today."

"That's one smart dog," observed Charlie. "He's looking after his horses and our interest."

So Monty joined the wagon train as their protector. The wagon master may have had his suspicions, but he never said anything more about pets either to Robert or to Charlie. Monty knew where he belonged and took up his position to guard his horses and his family.

By this time, the countryside had opened up. Farmland stretched out on either side of the road. The neat fields of corn and wheat planted in perfect rows showed that the owners were Pennsylvania Dutch. They kept their farms orderly and clean, the farmyards swept, and the barns were always painted red with decorations and hex signs on them. The Scots-Irish barns were also red or white, but without the decorations. Their houses had two chimneys, one at each end. The Pennsylvania Dutch houses had a single chimney in the middle, and the front door was off-center.

"You are very brave to have come out to America with your sister and your friends," Robert told Mrs. Glynis, one of the Welsh ladies whom Sarah had met. They walked down together to fill their water buckets at the creek.

"We wanted more opportunity to teach than Wales gave us, Mr. Jones. We asked my brother to take up the land grant and allow us to live on it, since women cannot own property. We also had a friend, Tom Harrison, who came to Winchester and found it more profitable than Wales. He is now in charge of one of the fifty schools in the Winchester area, and he got all four of us jobs for the autumn. We are looking forward to this year's teaching in America."

Mrs. Glynis had an adventuresome spirit. She appeared young, in her forties, and was eager for a new experience. Still attractive, with dark hair, blue eyes, and a slim figure, she had never remarried after her husband died in a coal mining accident.

"I could not remain in Wales, Mr. Jones. It had too many memories. I took a chance to get away to America," she continued as they sat beside the stream one day at lunch.

"Yes," said Robert. "I know how you felt. I needed to leave the mines. I hoped I could farm and make a new beginning in a new land."

Robert looked older than he was from his days in the mines. His dark hair was touched with grey, and his injured legs caused him to limp. He was in his middle forties and eager for a second chance. Robert's love of the countryside and his desire to learn a new trade made him curious about life in America. He was always happy to help Charlie with the horses, and Charlie showed him how to put on the harness with its complicated straps and buckles. Robert had never handled a four-horse hitch before, but he learned quickly. Charlie appreciated Robert's willingness to work and soon came to depend upon his help. They were up with the birds' dawn chorus before it was light, and were the last to go to bed. The lightning bugs, the tree toads, and the cicadas had long finished their evening songs and dances before the two men lay down to sleep.

## ANNIE AND ADAMS

Annie watched Charlie and her father handle the horses. "It must not be all that hard to learn to ride one of the wheelers," she told herself. "I'd love to learn."

One evening when Charlie led Washington and Adams to pasture, Annie asked him, "Will you teach me to ride Adams? Is he quiet enough?"

"These are workhorses, and they are not suitable for riding," Charlie told her. "You need a ladies' mount, not a workhorse."

But Annie would not be put off. When the horses were left in the pasture the following evening, she caught Adams and led him up to a board fence, which she climbed to boost herself onto his back. Carefully, she held the short lead she had tied to his halter like reins. Then she guided Adams around the pasture at a walk. It was twilight and nobody saw her, as most of the members of the wagon train were preparing supper.

For several evenings, Annie rode Adams around the field without being noticed. She taught herself how to guide him with the halter lead. Adams thought at first this was a new exercise, since he had pulled the wagon all day and was tired. But he didn't object and enjoyed the carrot Annie gave him after she slid off his back onto the ground.

One evening, when Robert failed to remove Adams's bridle, Annie rode him with a bit for the first time. She rode astride and was delighted in feeling the powerful horse underneath her. She guided him with the bridle, just as she had seen Charlie and her father do. Then she urged the tired horse into a slow trot, but it was bouncy, and she grasped Adams's thick mane to keep from falling.

After a short ride, Annie slid off the horse and gave him the carrot she hid in her pocket. Not wanting Charlie or her father to come to find her, Annie slipped the bridle from Adams's head and returned to the family circle. She usually rode until the lightning bugs appeared, because afterwards it became too dark, and her family went to bed when the mosquitoes got to biting.

"Is this Adams's bridle?" she inquired. "I found it still on him."

Annie rode Adams for another week before Charlie discovered her secret. He watched her one evening from the far end of the field. As she rode Adams at a walk, Charlie noted her natural ability and how easily she guided Adams at a slow trot down the fence line. Charlie said nothing to her until several days later.

"How did Adams behave?" he asked Annie one evening. "You are a pretty good horsewoman."

"How did you know?" Annie replied, startled by the unexpected question.

"I've watched you," Charlie said. "You have a natural ability, but you need a saddle and a riding bridle, not a work bridle with blinders. Let me see what I can find that's more suitable."

Charlie found a riding bridle at one of the German farms and shod a horse for the farmer to obtain it.

"Now," he told Annie, "you have the right equipment. All you still need is a saddle."

Annie continued to ride Adams bareback. Charlie taught her how to turn the horse and how to back him. Charlie also taught her proper voice commands and how to use her legs to put pressure on Adams's sides to make him turn to the right and left.

"Annie, even without a saddle, you are riding very well," he said.

## THE SUSQUEHANNA CROSSING

The countryside looked beautiful in July with the corn and wheat growing on either side of Lancaster Pike. The river crossing was not far off, as they had covered fifteen or twenty miles that day. Although the wagon train moved slowly, it went steadily westward.

Ed, the wagon master, debated whether to cross at Wright's Ferry or to go farther north to Harris's Ferry, which might be an easier crossing. He finally decided to save the horses and cross the Susquehanna at Lancaster County. The trip to Harris's Ferry was longer, and the crossing might be rougher because of the confluence of the Juniata River with the Susquehanna. The rivers were often in spate, and this made the crossing dangerous.

At Wright's Ferry, the Susquehanna was still wild and unpredictable, but with a lesser volume of water, it could be safer for horses and their heavily loaded wagons. The first eight wagons would cross in the afternoon until it got dark, and the second eight in the morning at sunup.

Ed decided this as he drove his team of four horses near the end of the wagon train. Tony, a young lad of sixteen, helped him and often ran errands for him.

"Tony, go tell the teamsters we will cross at Wright's Ferry and we will continue driving through Lancaster County to the river. Then we'll cross the Potomac in Maryland at Light's Ferry. I hope the Conestoga River isn't high because it feeds into the Susquehanna and adds to the amount of water we have to cross. There's been rain, because the corn looks well filled out, but not enough to make the ground soggy. It should be all right. Explain to the teamsters our plans and tell them to get ready to stay the night."

Tony rode his pony, Arrow, down the line of wagons to give the teamsters the message.

Before the wagon train reached the Susquehanna,

the Conestoga River curved around Lancaster, and the wagon train could either use a bridge or go over a ford. The Conestoga joined the Susquehanna near Wright's Ferry. The fords could be tricky when the river was in flood, but the horses did not like the new wooden covered bridge because it sounded hollow under their hooves. Jefferson snorted and shied when asked to cross it, so Charlie took the ford.

When they arrived at Wright's Ferry, the traffic to cross the river was heavy. This meant that the wagon train couldn't cross on the first afternoon, but had to until the next day.

"I was afraid of this delay, but it's better than going on to Harris's Ferry. That's a lot more risky," Ed told Charlie as he pulled his horses up beside Adams and Washington. "We'll be here overnight."

"When can we cross?" asked Charlie.

"Between the first and second bell tomorrow morning. There are several wagons ahead of us. The rivers are not high, and it should go smoothly. Let the quieter teams cross first—then you can take your team, since Jefferson gets nervous," Ed replied. "By the way, John Row isn't coming; one of his horses is lame, and he cannot use him. So he's in York and sent word by one of the packhorse men working on the road."

"I can finish the trip," Charlie said. "I didn't expect John to come after I learned his horse was lame. I know he hasn't got a spare one for an emergency."

"There is a boarding house in town if you want to stay the night there. Mrs. Rohr runs a clean establishment, and she has good food. She's on Elm Street, about six blocks from the river. Robert can stay there, too, since he's married to Sarah. It might be better if you slept there tonight. I'll take care of your horses and Monty, Annie's dog. Tony's taken quite a fancy to him."

Charlie didn't reply until he caught his breath. "Yes,

a bed would be nice for a change. Can you manage all those horses?"

"I have Tony, remember. He would love to look after your team. He's also crazy to have a hound dog. Go look after your people, Charlie. I'll see the team is taken care of all right."

Robert and Charlie felt relieved. They were both tired, and Robert still had to take care of Sarah.

"What will Ed say about my dog?" ask Annie, uneasy about trusting Monty with him even for the night.

"Don't worry, Annie, he knows about your pet. Ed has two teams to take care of, and one hound won't cause him any trouble. He'll find out how nice a dog Monty really is. Tony will look after him, and you can sleep in a nice clean bed."

They walked the six blocks to Mrs. Rohr's well-cared-for boarding house. First, Sarah had a bath, and by sundown, she was asleep. Annie and Ellen soon followed her to bed, and Robert wasn't far behind after a visit to Wright's Tavern.

Meanwhile, Tony played with Monty and took care of Charlie's fine team. Ed was unhappy about the delay because he felt sure that the crossing would not be finished until sundown the next day. They could not travel in the dark, so that would be two days lost.

At noon the next day, the first teams of Ed's wagon train crossed over the Susquehanna. They seemed to have little trouble, but Ed wanted to be sure before he told Charlie to cross with his team.

"How high is the water?" Ed asked the ferryman. "Is the current swift this morning?"

"Yes, quite swift, and it's strong. We need to cross the quiet teams before Charlie takes Jefferson over. He's not always dependable and can cause trouble if he's not handled right. There is stabling and a big pasture on the other side. Mr. Wright has opened a second tavern over there, too. It's not as big as the one on this side, but it's got new stables, and this tavern has better food."

After Ed watched the other teams cross with little trouble, he called Charlie. "Get your team ready to go next. The family will have to go later as foot passengers. Just the horses and the wagon go with you, and Robert can help look after them."

Charlie led Jefferson and Madison onto the ferry once it was unloaded of the pack animals crossing from the western side. The river flowed swiftly, but the horses seemed quiet and untroubled as Charlie led Jefferson onto the raft. Robert took Madison and unhitched the leaders from Adams and Washington. The four horses stood quietly, and the ferryman put up the tailgate. Then the boat was set into motion and rowed across by the ferrymen. Robert held Washington and Adams, but they seemed unconcerned about the water's swooshing sound against the wooden boat.

The three ferrymen rowed the open craft away from the shore, and slowly the little boat headed for the deeper water in the channel. The ferry jerked as a wave hit it, and Jefferson jumped. Charlie held him.

"Whoa, whoa, there now. Stand still." Charlie offered the nervous horse a fresh carrot, which he eagerly chewed. "Here's one for Madison." Charlie handed Robert a second carrot.

The ferry, once in the channel, was taken swiftly down the river by the current. The ferrymen rowed the boat toward the opposite shore. Then, suddenly, the ferry turned out of the channel toward the western bank. Madison pushed against Robert as he became unbalanced. Robert steadied the leaning horse and set him on his feet once again. Neither was hurt nor alarmed by the sudden turn.

Jefferson was busy with his second carrot as he leaned on Charlie. He shuffled his feet and continued eating. Charlie held him tight and got him balanced on his feet once more. The boat landed safely, and the horses seemed unruffled.

"That's good," sighed Charlie. "We made that crossing easily enough."

"There's stabling over here and a big pasture," one of the ferrymen told them. "The livery man is Mr. Dean. Tell him I said to give your horses stabling. There are nice big stalls, and there is some newly cut hay as well."

The ferrymen secured the craft and told Robert and Charlie that they were now in York County, Pennsylvania.

Charlie and one of the men led Madison and Jefferson off the ferry, while Robert and a second ferryman helped take Adams and Washington ashore. The horses sniffed the air and snorted with happiness to be back on firm ground again.

"Wright's Tavern is about five hundred yards over to the right, and the stabling is behind it. I'll bring over the foot passengers so you have time to enjoy a meal and get the horses settled."

"Come on," said Charlie. "Let's find Mr. Dean and see that the horses are fed. Then we can enjoy our meal."

The ferryman loaded a wagon and a team of four horses onto his ferry for the return journey. In Wrightsville, across the river where Sarah and the girls waited with Monty to cross as foot passengers, they left their boarding house and headed for the ferry. It was now late afternoon, and both the girls and their mother were anxious to be reunited with Charlie and Robert. At the ferry landing, the foot passengers gathered to wait for the ferry's return to take them across to the western side of the Susquehanna.

Together with several other foot passengers, the girls and their mother waited impatiently for the ferry's return. It was nearly dinnertime when the family was reunited.

Monty hated the ferry and barked at the swooshing water. He was glad to be back on land and greeted Charlie with a wag of his tail and a cheerful bark.

"There is a nice boarding house in the town the lady from last night told us about. Mrs. Ilse Becker, I think she said. Mrs. Becker runs a good safe and clean place. I hope it's not all full," Ellen told her father. "Can we go and find it before it gets too late?"

Once they had gotten a place to stay and checked on the horses, Robert left Monty with Tony. Then he and his family took Charlie out for a meal. After a long day, they all went to bed early.

"We shall continue on to York in the morning," Ed told his teamsters. "Tony, go and tell the drivers that we'll go on until we find a pasture where we can stop."

Tony kicked his pony into a trot and delivered Ed's message to the men on the wagons.

"We are going toward the town of York," Tony told Charlie.

"Good," Charlie replied. "That will give my horses a chance to calm down. Jefferson got excited back there with all those horses and wagons. York is less busy. And no more rivers to cross."

"Not until we get to the Potomac," Tony said. "Then the fun begins because the Potomac can be wild."

"There are too many rivers that come together at the Potomac. At least we're not going to cross at Harper's Ferry. That's the worst, with the confluence of a branch of the Shenandoah with the Potomac," Charlie remarked. "We are almost home now."

The wagon train entered York County. The farms were still beautiful, but there were fewer of them. Most were owned by Pennsylvania Dutch and Scots-Irish farmers. Once Charlie and his team had caught up with the wagon train, Monty joined them again.

The next morning, Ellen went to investigate the roadside stands and discovered fresh vegetables and big ripe fruits. She chose several and inquired about the watermelon, which she had never seen before.

"It's an American fruit," the Scots-Irish farmer told her. "Very good, but be careful not to swallow the seeds."

"I'll take one," said Ellen.

"Here, let me help you carry it. Which wagon is yours?"

"The number two wagon over there," Ellen told him. "You're very kind and accommodating."

The farmer left the stand to his wife and daughter as he helped Ellen take her purchase to her surprised family.

"Whatever did you buy?" asked Robert.

"An American food I've never seen before. Have you ever heard of a watermelon?" Ellen replied.

"What is that?" Robert picked up the watermelon and thumped it. "And how do you eat it?"

"You crack it open and eat it raw," Ellen said.

"And what is this?" said Robert, opening a bag and taking out one of Annie's other strange purchases.

"It's called a sweet potato. The farmer told me that you can make a pie out of it."

"How can you make a pie out here in the wilderness?" Robert asked.

Charlie stuck his head around a tree trunk. "I'll get my friend Mrs. Dickson to make one. She lives about five or six miles from here. Then you can eat a sweet potato pie. A real American dish."

Charlie gave the bag of sweet potatoes to Tony and sent him ahead to ask Mrs. Dickson if she could make a pie. Charlie smiled at the thought of having such a treat on the long road to Winchester.

Tony took the sweet potatoes to Mrs. Dickson, who sent word for Charlie to stop by the next morning.

"Tell Charlie hello for me," she told him. "I'll be glad to see him again. My husband runs the tavern, and we've known Charlie for several years. We see him when he comes through with the wagon trains. I'll get a pie ready for him."

Mrs. Dickson didn't usually make pies for people passing through, but she knew Charlie because they had been neighbors a few years previously. A year ago, she had moved with her husband to his brother's farm, away from the Shenandoah Valley to just outside of York.

Mrs. Dickson hoped to see Charlie once again, so she agreed to his special request. Meanwhile, she offered Tony something to eat and sent him to stable his pony and to wait for the wagon train.

When the wagon train arrived later that evening, she welcomed Charlie into her front room.

"Hello," she greeted him. "You are a loose penny, always turning up in unexpected places. I have your pie ready. I hope your Welsh family likes it."

Mrs. Dickson brought forth a magnificent pie and offered this special American dish to her visitors.

"Oh," said Ellen. "It's beautiful!"

"Mmm," agreed Annie. "I've never eaten anything like it before."

"This is different," said Robert, "but very good. I ate watermelon yesterday for the first time, and I like it, too."

Even Sarah agreed that the pie tasted delicious. "America has some strange foods," she commented as she ate a second piece of sweet potato pie.

"It's a new adventure," Charlie told her. "But sometimes adventures can be fun."

After a short visit, Charlie felt that they had better be going. "Ed said the stop in York would be brief—only long enough to replace a broken harness. So, we need to be on our way."

## MONTY AND THE SKUNK

Sarah had never heard of a skunk. "We don't have such animals in Wales," she protested when Charlie told her about skunks, opossums, and raccoons.

"The 'possums play dead when they're in danger," Charlie explained, "and the mamas carry their young on their backs."

"Oh, Charlie, you do make up some wonderful stories." Sarah laughed as she joined him at breakfast.

"Be careful," Charlie warned her, "because the skunk sprays a stinking, suffocating odor if it's threatened. Make sure neither you nor Monty bother a black-and-white animal about the size of a small dog or cat. The skunk has a long bushy tail and ambles through the woods at a slow pace."

"Charlie, you are a great tease and storyteller," Sarah said. "Wherever do you get such ideas?"

A few days later, Monty and Sarah encountered their first skunk. Sarah discovered some birds in the woods near their campground, and she wanted to see them more closely. She'd never seen a cardinal or an American robin. She and Monty left their picnic lunch to walk in the woods near the stream.

"Come on, Monty," she called to the dog. "Let's go for a stroll."

Monty and Sarah took a path and followed it toward an old tree stump where a pair of bluebirds built their nest. In late July, the woods were alive with birdsong.

"I've never seen so many beautiful birds," Sarah told Monty as they walked on. "There are red ones and grey ones, and the bird I saw this morning was a brilliant blue with a red breast."

Monty followed Sarah and felt happy in the woods with their curious, earthy smells. He poked his nose into pine needles on the forest floor and inspected the bushes for the scent of other animals.

Monty raised his head when he saw a new creature amble through the trees. It appeared to be a cat, but Monty wasn't sure because it was black with white stripes and a long, bushy tail. It didn't run like a cat, or spit at him, but simply wandered across the forest floor minding its own business. This catlike creature was not a cat, but a skunk.

Monty's curiosity brought him too close, and the skunk let out its protective spray. The dog howled in pain, and Sarah covered her face and ran blindly, hoping to find the stream. Monty rolled in the dirt beside the water, yelping.

Although the skunk's spray hadn't touched her, Sarah nearly choked on the odor. Unable to call for help, her face wet with tears, Sarah took off her shoes and stockings and jumped into the water. Still, the odor suffocated her. Frantically, Sarah picked up the wet dirt and rubbed it on her legs and arms.

In the distance, Charlie recognized the skunk's smell. He felt alarmed when he saw that Sarah and Monty had not returned. He found a jug of vinegar among his tools and grabbed a baking soda pouch. Then, without telling anyone where he was going, Charlie entered the woods in search of Sarah and Monty. When he could not find either of them, he ran on. Then he saw the catlike creature amble at his leisurely pace into the deeper part of the forest.

"Oh, dammit," Charlie exclaimed out loud. "The devil take it! Sarah and Monty have got mixed up with a skunk."

Charlie followed the suffocating smell to the stream. Here he found the dog frantically rolling in the dirt, and Sarah, half-naked, in the water, crying. Charlie ran to her.

"What the dickens have you got into? Here, use this vinegar and soda, and the towel I've brought with me. I'll get you a quilt," he told Sarah before he ran back to the wagon.

Meanwhile, Robert and his girls ate lunch with Mrs. Glynis and Miss Gwynn at their campground. They remained unaware of the trouble at the stream, except for the strange odor carried by the light wind.

In the wagon, Charlie found a dress and some undergarments. He also grabbed a heavy quilt and ran back to Sarah and Monty.

"Oh, Charlie," cried Sarah, "what have I got into?"

"A skunk. You and Monty were sprayed by a skunk. Where did you find him?"

Charlie put the quilt around Sarah's shoulders. Although the skunk's spray hadn't hit her, she was shivering from cold and shock.

"I'm not dressed," she protested weakly as Charlie rubbed vinegar and dirt on her arms and legs.

"Here," Charlie said, "wash off the dirt and vinegar. Then put on these clothes. They're clean and dry."

Charlie turned his back to give Sarah privacy as she changed her clothes. He bundled up her soiled garments and the towel and threw them onto the opposite bank. Then he went to help Monty, who was still rolling in the mud and whimpering.

Monty was trying to rid himself of the skunk's spray. Charlie knew it would take about two weeks to get rid of the odor. He rubbed dirt and vinegar into the dog's fur and lifted the frightened animal into the tumbling water.

Finally, after an hour of rubbing dirt onto the whimpering dog, and with repeated washings, at last he and Sarah were able to return to the wagon and the horses. Charlie felt sure that Robert must be frantic wondering where his wife had gone.

Once again, Charlie got Sarah to rub herself with vinegar. He crossed the stream over a fallen log and buried her clothes, the quilt, and the towel. Monty hung his head and whined as if in pain when they walked through the woods back to the wagon.

"Where have you been?" Robert asked as Sarah and Charlie emerged from the forest. He sounded angry, although he felt relieved to see his wife unharmed. "What's that terrible smell?"

"Monty got sprayed by an animal called a skunk," Sarah explained, still in tears. "We can't get rid of the smell."

"Phew! Why can't you get rid of it?" Robert asked.

"What is that terrible smell?" Annie cried as she backed away from her mother.

Charlie tried to explain what happened. "It's taken a whole hour for us to become this presentable. Poor Monty still smells bad."

Robert took Sarah's hand and led her toward their picnic table. "Come on, dear, let's have something to eat." Sarah finally dried her tears and accepted a cup of tea.

Later that afternoon, Ed crossed the pasture to comfort Sarah. "You'll be all right," he told her. Ed found a Mennonite family from whom he purchased a quilt to replace the one Charlie buried, and gave it to Sarah.

"This is for you," he said, presenting her with the brightly colored quilt, decorated with geometric figures.

Sarah was overwhelmed by such kindness and burst into a new cascade of tears.

"Thank you, Ed," she whispered. "It's a beautiful quilt. Thank you."

Mrs. Glynis and Miss Gwynn offered all kinds of scents and even got some parsley from a farmer to rub on Sarah's arms to reduce the lingering skunk odor.

Poor Monty—in spite of Charlie's washing him in milk, vinegar, baking soda, and everything else that the teamsters and the immigrants suggested—it took two weeks before he was again accepted in polite company.

## THE POTOMAC CROSSING

Several days later, as the wagon train turned toward Hagerstown from Gettysburg, it began to rain. Ellen and Robert helped Charlie close the Conestoga wagon's curtains. Eventually, the summer showers developed into a frightening storm.

"It's soaked the bedding," cried Ellen. "Annie, come help me move the blankets from the front seat!"

Charlie held the horses steady as rain swept over them, soaking his team and their leather harness. The water made the reins slippery. Jefferson became fractious and began to canter. He hated the rain in his ears. Madison also broke into a canter and tried to kick Adams behind him.

The rain bucketed down, and a strong wind lashed at the family, now huddled in the wagon. Robert, soaking wet, walked beside the frightened horses.

"Robert, take Jefferson's head and see if he will walk and stop the cantering," Charlie shouted over the storm.

Robert did as Charlie asked, but Jefferson refused to walk. The other horses became rambunctious as the teamsters tried to calm them. Lightning flashed around them, and thunder rattled in the sky. Monty hid in the wagon, and Jefferson leapt forward as if all the witches of the storm chased him.

Finally, outside Gettysburg, they came to a big farm. "Go into the pasture by that barn," commanded Ed, as the situation with the frightened horses became more serious. The barn had a middle aisle and a number of stalls. It belonged to Gordon Kennedy, who raised draft horses.

As the wagon train moved toward his pasture, Gordon met them. "Ed, get your horses under cover. This thunder sounds wicked."

Ed guided his teams toward an enormous red barn. He yelled for everyone to follow him.

Gordon and his four sons opened the big double doors. "Catch that chestnut, Brian," he said to his son as a big clap of thunder nearly deafened them. "He's about to jump out of his skin. He's scared of thunder,"

Jefferson stood on his hind legs, and Brian caught his bridle and led the frightened animal down the long hallway to the back of the barn. "Now, you behave," Brian told Jefferson as he brought Charlie's team to a halt.

"There are twenty-five box stalls and ten standing ones," Gordon Kennedy told the teamsters. "Now you can get your horses settled."

"What a blessing to have shelter," said Annie, as she jumped from the wagon with Monty.

"Charlie, do you want a loose box or a standing stall?" Robert asked.

"We can put two horses in a loose box if we tie them," Charlie said. "Get this wet harness off and hang it over the stall doors to dry."

"Whoa, Jefferson, stand still," Brian commanded as lightning flashed and thunder made the horses jump.

The teamsters un-harnessed their frightened animals and, after rubbing them down with dry sacking, the men led them into the waiting stalls.

"What a storm!" cried Sarah. "The whole earth is shaking." She stood up in the wagon bed and shivered with fear, her hair wild and her clothes soaked.

"We're safe and warm now," Annie told her. "Our blankets are damp, but we're all right. Even Monty is happy to be inside."

Sarah stood in the wagon shivering and cried. Ellen threw the wet contents of the wagon onto the barn floor.

"Charlie, are we to sleep in the wagons?" Robert asked, worried about his family's safety.

"Yes, but take out the rest of the wet things," Charlie answered. "There's dry hay and straw to put on the floor of the wagon."

Outside, the storm raged and thunder shook the barn, but the occupants were soon warm and dry as they huddled around a Franklin stove in the large tack room at the rear of the barn.

The morning dawned clear and cool. The Monocacy River now appeared dangerous. Ed worried about the situation at the Potomac, at Light's Ferry. He was afraid of an accident.

"I don't know whether we should try a crossing," he told the teamsters. "The storm last night dumped a lot of water. We have to cross the Potomac, and it's the most dangerous of all the rivers."

"We can manage," one of the teamsters said. "I've done it many times, and it's no problem."

"That storm last night bucketed rain," said Charlie. "It could be very dangerous."

"We'll wait a while," said Ed. "We'll try to cross by Light's Ferry as usual. In another hour, we'll harness the horses and get ready to leave the barn. By then, the sun will have dried out the road."

Outside, branches and leaves lay scattered across the pastureland. The corn was bent and broken, and several shingles from the barn's roof had torn loose and lay on the ground. It felt cold for late July.

"It's not going to be easy to cross any river today," observed Charlie. "I don't like the looks of the sky."

Ed waited until mid-morning before the wagon train began to follow the path of the Monocacy River east of Antietam Creek across Maryland toward Virginia.

Several trees had been struck by lightning. Their branches crisscrossed the ground and blocked their way. The debris was scattered everywhere and created a pattern, like some kind of crazy patchwork quilt. Jefferson shied at the skeletal branches, but Charlie held him firm. The teamsters guided their horses across the battered landscape as Ed decided what to do.

"This is a poor day to travel," Charlie told Robert. "It's taking an awful risk."

"Where are we going?" Annie asked. "All I can see are damaged and soggy fields."

"We are going to cross the Potomac River from Maryland into Virginia," Charlie told her. The empty and storm-ravaged landscape troubled him. He studied the sky to see if more rain might be on its way, noting that the dark clouds had built up once again.

After two hours of slow and hazardous driving over damaged roads, the wagons reached the Potomac. The river, now in spate, swept by them at a rapid pace. The water tumbled over the rocky shore, carrying broken fences and tree limbs with it.

Mr. Light, the ferryman, shook his head. "I can't take you across now. It's too dangerous," he insisted. "The ferry will be swamped."

"Can we use the ford?" Ed asked.

"No, the horses don't like the swirling noise, and the ferry isn't stable enough to take your teams across just now," Mr. Light replied. "Wait until morning, and we'll see what she's like then. The Potomac is an unpredictable old lady at the best of times, and today she is definitely furious."

"I agree," said Charlie. "It's too dangerous. The ford is too deep to cross with a loaded wagon."

Ed was anxious to go on and didn't want to add more days to the journey, but Mr. Light shook his head. "No," he said firmly. "You will have to wait."

A disappointed Ed drew his wagons into a big pasture. The teams were unhitched and tethered to graze.

Charlie drove his horses down to the far end of the field away from the others. Here, he and Robert unhitched the wagon and took the harness off their frightened team. The horses drank water from buckets. Then Robert tethered the animals to spend the day resting.

"I need to reset Washington's shoes," Charlie told Robert as he looked for his supplies. "I'll get my anvil and tools if you'll hold the horse. The shoes he has on are almost worn through."

Annie and Ellen helped their mother down from the wagon, and they found a dry place under two large chestnut trees where they could watch Charlie work. Robert held the big horse while Charlie pulled Washington's old shoes off and put on new ones. Washington stood quietly while Charlie trimmed his hooves and fitted the new metal shoes. The horse sniffed the top of Charlie's hair and seemed to appreciate the attention to his feet. Washington decided the red hair was not good to eat and tossed his head as if to express his disappointment.

Afterward, Charlie worked on Madison, who was a bit touchy. He blew and snorted as Charlie cleaned his feet and checked his shoes for loose nails. Madison objected when Charlie replaced a nail and filed down his hooves. The heavy atmosphere made the horses feel edgy. Madison jumped suddenly and broke his tether. Annie led the big horse back to Charlie, who retied the lead.

"He's a bit skittish," Charlie explained. "He doesn't like anyone to bother his feet, but he's all right. It's Jefferson who's really ticklish."

Jefferson stood still because Robert offered him a carrot, and the horse was distracted as he ate it. "He's all right today. He has something to take his attention from his feet. He loves carrots," Robert said, as he gave Jefferson a pat and offered him a second carrot. Annie had found the carrots at a roadside stand in Gettysburg.

Charlie returned to the forge, and Ellen gave Washington and Adams each a carrot. When Charlie finished resetting their shoes, he turned the horses out to graze in the pasture.

Meanwhile, Sarah fell asleep under the trees, while Annie decided to make a cup of tea. "I was sure the canister was almost empty," she told her sister, "but today it's full of tea. There is truly something magic about this teapot. It never runs out of tea."

Charlie put away his tools, and after dousing the fire in his forge, he and Robert joined the girls under the trees for some refreshment. Ellen had found a pastry shop in Gettysburg that sold teacakes and German *kuchen*. These she now offered to her father and Charlie to eat with their tea. The men chatted together, eager to plan Robert's future farm. While Sarah took a brief nap, Ellen and Annie went with Monty for a walk.

The four Welsh ladies, Mrs. Glynis, her sister, Miss Gwynn, and two other teachers from South Wales, had camped nearby, and the girls went to visit them.

"We've just come to say hello," Annie called, holding Monty on a lead in case he bounded over the grass to greet the Welsh ladies with his wet kisses.

Ellen offered them some of her Gettysburg cakes and cookies. "They are German *kuchen*, or little cakes, and they're very good," she explained, passing them to the four ladies. "Ed told me that in America, coffee is drunk now more often than tea. I have some coffee also. Would you like to try some? Charlie told me it comes from Brazil in South America."

"I tried some coffee once," Miss Gwynn said. "It's all right, but I prefer my cup of tea."

"How are you girls getting on?" asked Mrs. Glynis. "Do you know when we will cross the river? It looks much too rough this afternoon."

"We shall wait until tomorrow morning when it might be less dangerous," Ellen replied. "Charlie, our teamster, re-shod the horses so they won't slip on the ferry. He said when the water is rough, worn shoes are slippery and can cause an accident."

"So we are using the delay to prepare for the crossing. Mr. Light seems to think that later this afternoon it will be less windy and so the water will be less dangerous," Annie said as she offered the ladies each another German cake.

"It's a long and perilous trip to Virginia. I'm very worried about the rapids and turbulent water," Mrs. Glynis told them.

"What brought you to America, Mrs. Glynis?" Annie asked. She sat down beside the older woman as they gathered for their tea. Annie preferred not to think of crossing the Potomac.

"I wanted a different life after my husband died," she explained. "I am a teacher, and I thought I could find work more easily in Virginia than in Wales, so I came with my sister, Gwynn, and two of her friends. In Wales, it is not easy for a woman teacher without a husband. Gwynn said her friend who came to Winchester some years ago has done well there. She suggested I come out with my sister and our friends. We consider it a great adventure to be pioneers seeking new lands and new ways of living. Since women can't own property, my brother took up the land grant."

Annie and Ellen were amazed at the bravery of these four women, and it made the girls feel that they might do unusual things. After visiting a little longer, the sisters took their leave and headed back toward their wagon with Monty. "It's amazing what women do these days," Annie remarked. "Fancy coming all this way alone to begin a new life."

The next morning the Potomac looked less angry, and Mr. Light gave instructions about the crossing.

"First," he said, "we shall take the quieter teams and wagons. The wagons will be brought on to the ferry and chocks placed in front of the wheels. The teams will be unhooked from their wagons. A teamster and one helper will go with them; after that, the heavier wagons will cross, and then the foot passengers will go together—last."

Ed brought up the quieter horses, and the ferrymen carefully loaded their craft. The wind dropped and the first wagon and its horses crossed over safely. The crossing was rough, but the team stood still and the wagon didn't move, so the ferry was well balanced.

The ferrymen skillfully brought the boat over the rough and swirling water. On the far side of the Potomac, the horses and wagons were reunited and left the ferry safely. Once in Virginia, the teamsters found that Mr. Light owned a second house and a tavern with stabling, where the men and horses were accommodated until the rest of the wagon train crossed. The crossing lasted all day, but Mr. Light was determined to have no accidents and took his time.

Slowly, Charlie led Jefferson, and Robert led Madison onto the ferry. They were unhitched and the wagon secured. The ferrymen started to cross the fast-flowing, debris-filled water.

Charlie kept the horses quiet as they headed for the Virginia shore. The swishing and swooshing sound of the water startled Jefferson, and he danced on the ferry's wooden deck. Charlie held the nervous horse and offered him a carrot, but this time Jefferson wasn't interested. *Swoosh, swirl, swoosh* went the water, and the skittish horse shied at the strange sounds. A log scraped the ferry's side.

"Hold on, Jefferson," Charlie said. "The water is not going to hurt you."

Madison pawed the floorboards and became more restive as the ferrymen reached the midpoint of the journey across the Potomac. All four horses danced a little jig even though both Robert and Charlie tried to quiet them.

The river was full of trash from the storm. Tree branches caught against the ferry's sides and banged against its wooden body. Jefferson snorted and danced with his feet in place. "Whoa, Jefferson," Charlie said. "We are nearly there."

Finally the swish and swoosh sounds were accompanied by a rattle that made the leaders jump. Charlie held Jefferson, but Robert tripped and fell in front of Madison, who tried to leap to one side. Charlie caught the horse's bridle and held him tight until Robert stood up and took hold of Madison again.

The ferry jerked and rattled, but the team stood firm. Charlie tried to quiet Jefferson as the ferry reached the opposite shore. Slowly the ferry docked, but a sudden gust of wind made the boat hit the bank with a jolt as the ferrymen secured it. Jefferson leapt forward and fell to his knees. Charlie pulled him up, but not before Jefferson cut himself and blood ran down his front legs.

Once the ferry was secure, the ferryman took Jefferson's bridle and guided the injured horse onto the south shore of the Potomac. Here, Charlie unhitched Jefferson and led him into a small paddock near Mr. Light's Tavern where he could clean the horse's bleeding knees. Robert led off the other horses and tethered them to a large tree.

"What a mess," said Charlie. "You are a fine one for foolishness," he murmured to the injured Jefferson as he patted his head.

"He's just skinned. The cuts don't look deep," one of the ferrymen commented. "It was a bad morning for a crossing. What's wrong with Ed's judgment? I'll leave you now and bring over the rest of the teams and passengers."

Charlie cleaned Jefferson's cuts and put some baking soda on them. Then he allowed the horses to settle down before he hitched them back again to the wagon.

"We'll leave them tied," Charlie told Robert. "I'm going to Light's Tavern for something to eat."

It took all day for the teams to cross the river. Some horses refused to go on the ferry and had to have their eyes covered. This caused more time to be lost, and it was sunset before the last team and wagon were safely over the river.

"Mr. Light says we can spend the night in his tavern," Ed told the teamsters.

"I don't want to go to the pub," Sarah told Robert. "It's full of men drinking."

"There's a private parlor for ladies," Charlie reassured her before he went off with several teamsters to enjoy his evening.

The Welsh ladies joined Sarah, Ellen, and Annie, and entered the ladies parlor for their dinner. Soon after the meal, tired and sore from their long day, the women retired to their wagons for some much needed sleep.

Monty lay down under the stars and snored contentedly. Perhaps he dreamt of chasing rabbits along the Virginia side of the river.

When Robert and Charlie came back from Light's Tavern, the camp was asleep.

The horses, now free in the ferryman's pasture, nibbled the grass and ate their rations of corn and oats. The July moon shone bright and full over the quiet land.

The next morning at sunup, Charlie started a fire and cooked himself some breakfast. He watched the dawn stars burn away as the sun rose and the birds in the trees called to one another. Slowly the camp came to life while Charlie fed and watered his horses. At sunrise, most people ate their breakfast. By the first bell, the teams were hitched to their wagons. The crows gathered to enjoy the leavings of the travelers' breakfast.

The corner of Virginia where they had camped lay peacefully before them. A rooster crowed. The day broke clear and fine—the storm clouds had dissipated—and the temperature began to warm up on a perfect summer morning.

Once again, the horses and teamsters took their places in line. Now that they were in Virginia, the immigrants were eager to see what lay ahead. The wagon train left the unpredictable Old Lady Potomac behind as the teams made their way into the Shenandoah Valley and on toward Winchester.

"We are almost at Winchester," Charlie announced to Annie and Ellen. "Just another two days or maybe three and we've made it." He felt relieved to have guided his passengers safely over the three weeks' trek.

Even Monty was frisky when he and the girls reached the Virginia side of the Potomac River. Only Sarah appeared glum and unhappy.

From Light's Ferry to Winchester was about fifty miles, but the going proved rough, and the road, although old and well maintained, was in the mountains.

"It is a pretty drive through the Shenandoah Valley—'land of the stars,' the Indians call it," Charlie told them. "If you keep a sharp lookout, you could see whitetail deer and hear the quail singing 'bob-white' and the whippoorwills calling to each other."

Although Jefferson's knees were stiff, he pricked his ears forward as if eager to head for home. Soon the horses would return to Charlie's farm and rest in his pasture. The wheelers, Washington and Adams, walked with a new spring in their steps. Their ears pricked forward as they looked for familiar landmarks along the way. Monty, now smelling less like skunk, took his usual place beside Adams.

"They know we are near home," Robert remarked, and the wagon train slowly made its way toward Winchester. "The whole company seems eager to press on."

As the horses and wagons drove toward Valley Road, which ran south into the Carolinas, Robert took out his crwth (pronounced "crowd," a traditional Welsh stringed instrument) and sang a Celtic song.

"I know that tune," remarked Johnny, the boy who drove the horses in the front wagon. He got out his dulcimer and played a mountain version of the same tune. It was simpler, with fewer notes, but the music was recognizable, although played differently.

Robert walked beside Madison, singing the Welsh version while Johnny played the mountain one. Charlie sang in a rhythmic way. Monty joined in with a *howl, howl, howl*.

Annie and Ellen laughed, and even Sarah sang with merriment. She took the crwth and bow from Robert, and played a bit of the tune. Sarah knew how to play the instrument well, but suddenly she felt embarrassed and gave the crwth back to Robert.

Johnny played his dulcimer by plucking. Robert was reminded of a zither he had once seen in a shop in Cardiff. He learned that Johnny's instrument was made by his grandfather, John Wilson, who was an accomplished musician. They lived near Winchester, and Mr. Wilson made traditional mountain instruments.

Johnny explained why they were on this wagon train. "We joined to bring my aunt and uncle across from Philadelphia to live with us until they can get their own farm."

"How did the bells work?" Charlie asked him. "You can keep them. I found another strap of bells in my tool box."

"That's grand! Ours must have fallen off when the buckle broke. We've never found them," Johnny replied. He continued to pluck the dulcimer and played "Barbara Allen" with some skill while his grandfather accompanied him on the fiddle. Uncle Iain, meanwhile, drove their team of four bay-colored horses.

"It's a cheerful sound to hear bells. It's always good to know when another team is coming along the road," John Wilson said. He was an older man who made very little small talk. He was not unfriendly, just more interested in his own thoughts. He was making a new dulcimer in his spare moments. Johnny did most of the work with their wagon and team, since his aunt and uncle spoke Scots-Gaelic and knew little English. His uncle, Iain, though, did help with the horses. Johnny's Aunt Bess was a silent, often depressed woman who preferred to remain alone. To amuse themselves, Johnny and his grandfather played their homemade instruments and sang the old folk songs but with different tunes and sometimes with mountain settings.

The farms they passed appeared as clean and neat as the ones they had seen in Pennsylvania's Dutch country, and they looked just as prosperous. There were red Devon cattle in the fields and some riding horses, not just heavy workhorses. The houses, often built of stone with two chimneys, were called "I" houses because of each chimney's resemblance to a capital "I." There was grass in the yards, and corn, wheat, and flax grew in the fields.

The wagons continued on to Winchester. Charlie drove his team through the valley to Red Bud Run. He was happy to learn from a farmer they met that the bridge was at last completed.

"Good," he told the farmer. "Maybe my horses won't get hurt. What's the water level like? Is it flooded or dangerous?"

"Not too bad. Just be careful going over the bridge. It can be slippery," the farmer replied.

"That's good to know. One of my horses got hurt coming over on the ferry. I don't need any more accidents," said Charlie.

"You should be all right," the farmer assured him. "The new bridge is well built and strong. Your horses should have a safe crossing."

Monty growled at the farmer's dog, and Ellen tied a lead to the hound's collar. "That's enough out of you, Monty. That dog's going about his business and doesn't need you to interfere."

"Lovely dog," the farmer remarked. "Looks like a

good hunting dog."

"He's also a guard dog," Annie replied. "He thinks he's the boss. Charlie hopes he can hunt and isn't gun-shy."

"Monty has a mind of his own," Charlie commented as they continued down the road. "I feel better about crossing the creek over a bridge. We are not far from Winchester now."

"No," the farmer agreed. "Good luck to you."

Charlie thanked him as the farmer and his shepherd dog moved toward their home across the field where sheep nibbled at the green grass.

The wagons slowly continued on their way to Winchester and beyond, and although Jefferson's knees were stiff, he kept up all right. Charlie didn't push him as the sixteen wagons made their way toward the new bridge.

The creek flowed quickly, but the bridge was high and the floor was not covered with water. The swirling sound of the creek was all that might scare the horses.

Charlie said, "After we cross, we'll wait in the pasture on the other side until everyone gets over."

"Good," said Joe, one of the teamsters. "Then we can get something to eat. There's a tavern another hundred yards down the road. I hope it's open."

Although the water appeared swift and some debris had collected on the bridge's supports, the horses stepped onto it with confidence. Charlie allowed his team to take the middle position, with other teams before and behind them.

Jefferson sniffed once, but he entered the covered bridge without any further trouble.

"Robert," called Charlie, "get ahold of Madison's bridle and make sure he is steady on the planking. It's not loose, is it?"

"No, it is nailed down. The bridge appears sound, so the horses should be all right."

This time they crossed without incident and pulled

into the pasture beside the road.

"I wish all crossings were that easy," Ed said with a sigh of relief.

"Some people don't have good judgment," Charlie snapped as he put more baking soda on Jefferson's stiff knees.

"I'm sorry that your horse got hurt, but the Potomac was big and wild, and the ferry was rough," Ed admitted grudgingly. He hated to have a horse or a person injured on his wagon trains.

Charlie might have said more, but Robert caught his arm. "Leave it," Robert said. "Jefferson's not badly injured—no need to start a fight. Didn't you say we only have twelve miles left to Winchester?"

Robert handed the reins to Annie and Ellen. "Look after the horses for us," he said. "We'll not be long." Then he and Charlie went to the tavern to cool off while the teamsters assembled their horses and stopped for something to eat.

Half an hour later, Charlie's tousled red hair appeared in the crowd of horses and wagons. He and Robert went back to their team and avoided an encounter with Ed on the way. "My mother told me to leave it where the Lord flung it," Charlie remarked, climbing up on his wagon.

"Our journey is almost over," Robert said. "Only one more day. The road seems well built, and we should make good time."

Charlie checked Jefferson's knees once more and, satisfied they were all right, got his horses fed and watered for the last part of the journey to Winchester.

# VIRGINIA

Ellen and Annie watched with eager anticipation as the big horses drew the wagons forward into the Valley of the Shenandoah River. The mountains, first the Blue Ridge, and beyond, the Appalachians, and finally the Alleghenies, surrounded them. Their father was happy sitting on the hard board seat of the Conestoga wagon and holding the reins of Charlie's four chestnut horses. The mountains and valley looked beautiful, and Robert felt that they could face life in America with confidence.

Only Sarah felt no excitement as the wagon train headed for Frederick County and Winchester. She was not looking forward to the new life that lay ahead of them. She sat next to her husband and started to cry.

"I want to go back to Wales," she wept. "I don't like this country; it's too big."

"It's the beginning of the Shenandoah Valley," Ellen told her mother. "It's beautiful land. The Indians called it the 'daughter of the skies.'"

"What if no one here speaks Welsh? The four ladies on the wagon train are the only people I've met who speak my language," Sarah insisted.

"Then you must learn to speak English," Robert told her. "We've come all this way into a very fertile valley with land to farm. What more could we wish for?"

"The valleys of South Wales," Sarah retorted. "That's what I dream about!"

Charlie walked beside his team holding on to Jefferson's bridle as they crossed the valley floor. Monty trotted alongside, his tail held high, sniffing the clear morning air.

"Don't worry," Charlie assured Sarah. "Once you get your land and house built, you'll find the valley a wonderful place to live."

The wagon train entered Winchester at noon the

next day. On the outskirts of the town, Mr. Duncan, who owned the general store and was on the town council, had set up a table under some shade trees. On the table, he had laid out a pile of papers for the new people now coming up the road toward him. Robert jumped down from the wagon and approached the table.

"Are you Mr. Duncan?" he asked.

"Yes," replied the man as he settled rocks on his piles of papers to keep them from blowing away.

"I'm Robert Jones from South Wales. I have applied for a land grant."

Mr. Duncan held out his hand in greeting.

"Welcome. I'm Isaac Duncan. Have you ever worked on a farm before?"

"No. I was a miner in the Welsh valleys until I had an accident," Robert replied. "I was injured and can't mine coal anymore."

"Then you'll need some help," Mr. Duncan said. "We have two good men who can help you settle in. Old Cyrus is a craftsman—he's good at building anything. The other is an Indian lad of twenty who was raised by the local doctor. Spotted Deer is apprenticed to Cyrus."

Robert listened, interested to learn more about the help Mr. Duncan offered.

"Go to the tavern in town and ask for Will Holliday, who owns it. He's a Scot from your part of the world. Will has a cabin behind the tavern where Old Cyrus and Spotted Deer live."

Mr. Duncan handed Robert the necessary papers and said, "When you talk to Will, he'll fix you up with accommodations."

Robert thanked him and went back to the wagon to get his belongings and his family. Annie had made a small fire and boiled water for tea. Granny's teapot sat on a rock beside the fire, and, near it, Annie laid five cups, milk, and sugar. Monty lay on the ground beside her, and wagged his tail as Robert came up.

"We're going to have to decide what to do with him," Robert said. "A dog right now will be difficult to handle. Maybe once we get settled in our own home, we can bring him back."

"I can take Monty with me," Charlie suggested. "I live in New Town, which is a hoot and a holler down the road from here. I could keep him for a while. My son would love a friendly dog like Monty. I'm sure my wife would be delighted, as my hound dog Prince is getting old."

"I hate to give Monty up," said Annie. "After all, I claimed him as mine."

"I understand, but we'll have to stay in a boarding house while we build a cabin, so it will be a while before we are ready to take care of a dog," Robert explained.

"New Town is up Valley Road, only about six miles away. I'll give Monty back to you when it's convenient for your family," Charlie assured her.

Annie said nothing, but she took her cup and walked away from the fire and her tea-making things. She stood alone at the edge of the gathering place. Several other wagons had stopped, and the men were consulting with Mr. Duncan at his table. Most of those people stopping in Winchester were either Scots-Irish or German Lutherans, but she overheard a few English families and one Welsh family.

Charlie tied a horse lead onto Monty's collar and led him away from the fire. "I'll take him," Ellen said, and led Monty toward the woods.

Meanwhile, Annie drank her tea in silence while her parents prepared their own. She had never owned a dog before, and she loved this nondescript hound. He was hers, not Charlie's. She was the one who had found Monty with his foot bleeding and bathed it in the stream.

"It won't be long," Charlie reassured her. "If he comes home with me, I'll bring him back to you when you are better able to look after him. I'll give you my address, and you can always ask for Charlie Smithson at the general store, and Mr. Fletcher, who owns it, will know how to find me."

"But I feel like I'm abandoning him, and I just found him," Annie replied, nearly in tears.

"One or two months, three months at most before you'll pick him up," Charlie encouraged the girl. "He loves you, Annie; I'll make a poor substitute."

Annie knelt down beside Monty and hugged him. Then she examined his foot. It had healed and was just a little sore. Charlie waited a few feet away. Nobody spoke while Annie explained the new arrangement to Monty, more to reassure herself than to comfort him. Then she led the dog to Charlie. Adams nuzzled her, looking for carrots, and Annie patted his neck. "I'll miss you, too, old boy."

She turned to Charlie. "Write down your address and the name of the man at the store in New Town."

Charlie did so and handed the piece of paper to her. "It's not far from town, near a big Lutheran German farm. The owner's name is Joseph Krauss, and he speaks English."

Charlie shook Robert's hand in farewell. Then the red-haired teamster lifted the surprised Monty onto the seat of the wagon and climbed up beside him. Tears ran down Annie's cheeks as she waved Charlie good-bye.

"See you all soon! Take care of yourselves," Charlie called, as he turned his horses back onto the road and headed south toward New Town.

The other teams followed. Annie watched them leave to meet the wagon train. She felt sad and lonely without Charlie and Monty. Several of the other teams were also from nearby towns and had not far to go. The main wagon train had gone earlier. Now, Robert and his family were near Winchester on their own.

A line formed at Mr. Duncan's table as more

settlers came to see about their papers. Suddenly, out of the crowd appeared an Indian youth. He approached Robert.

"I'm Spotted Deer. Mr. Duncan said you would need help into Winchester. I am to take you and several other people to Mr. Will Holliday's Tavern. We will use Mr. Duncan's wagon. It's parked over there behind that row of trees in the shade." The lad pointed to a farm wagon drawn by two brown horses that waited patiently and flicked flies from their backs with their long tails.

Annie looked at the swarthy young man in fear, and took Ellen's arm. She bundled her tea-making things together as if to protect them. To her amazement, Spotted Deer poured water from their bucket and doused the fire.

He explained again that Mr. Duncan sent him to help Robert's family get into Winchester, and that he would take them to Will's Tavern.

"To a tavern!" Sarah protested. "To a drinking man's tavern!"

"It's an eating place, too, and a place to stay, even for ladies like you," Spotted Deer replied.

Will Holliday, a Scots-Irishman from County Down in Northern Ireland, owned one of the several taverns in Winchester. Will's Tavern was on the main street and was a well-known stopping off place for travelers going both north and south. His tavern was the staging place for the public coaches and the stop where they changed horses. The Presbyterian Church objected to selling spirits on Sundays, but in order to stay in business, Will broke the church's rules to accommodate the travelers. Will's Tavern remained a popular venue, and he was held in high regard in spite of his relations with the Scottish church.

Spotted Deer drove the horses and wagon, which was a vehicle large enough to carry Robert's family and their bundles. A second Welsh couple, who also planned to settle in Winchester, joined them.

Robert introduced himself to the Welshman and his

wife. "I'm very happy to see you," he told them. "We didn't know if there would be anyone in Winchester who spoke our language, and my wife, Sarah, will be especially pleased."

"We're glad to meet you, too," said the man. "My name is Yorweth Llewellyn, and this is my wife, Blodwen. We come from South Wales also, where I used to be a miner."

With Spotted Deer driving them, the Welsh families entered Winchester in a certain amount of style. Will's Tavern was on the main street. The town, laid out in half-acre lots with its neat stone-and-frame houses, looked well kept. Will Holliday welcomed the tired travelers and offered them a place to sit in his private dining room. Sarah, exhausted after almost a month on the road from Philadelphia, sat down in an easy chair and immediately fell asleep.

Robert and Yorweth left the private dining room and entered the bar. Meanwhile, Ellen introduced herself to Blodwen, and they sat together with Annie to have a chat. She learned that Yorweth and Blodwen had no children and had decided to come to America after a long strike in one of the Welsh mines.

"We wanted to come out to America before we had any obligations," explained Blodwen.

"We came because my father was injured in a mining accident. He can no longer go down in the pit because of his legs," Ellen explained. "We've taken a land grant of one hundred acres."

"I understand the Shenandoah Valley is very fertile, and the farms are productive," Blodwen told them. "We also hope to take up a hundred acres."

Knowing that his family needed a place to live while a cabin was built and a barn erected, Robert asked Will Holliday if he knew of a boarding house in town where the family could stay.

"Yes, down this street, and on Piccadilly, the second street to your left, is Mrs. Taylor's. She runs a very good establishment. You can stay with her while you get your land ready for habitation. Tell Mrs. Taylor that I sent you to her. There should be no trouble getting a room."

He explained to Robert more about the land grant, and pointed out that it was west of town near the mountains, but not as far as Back Creek. "You'll need Old Cyrus and Spotted Deer to help build a dwelling and a barn."

Robert signed the paper for the land grant and asked when he could see the property.

"Spotted Deer will take you out there. It's not far, and it is a beautiful site. Then you should meet Old Cyrus because he's the best builder we have, and the best storyteller, too. He's a Revolutionary War veteran and fought at Cowpens with General Daniel Morgan. General Morgan also came from Winchester, and is buried here in the local cemetery. Old Cyrus will entertain you as you go out to see your property."

Robert thanked him and went back with Yorweth to finish his drink. The two men talked of the old country and spoke Welsh together. Yorweth and Blodwen also planned to stay at Mrs. Taylor's house.

With Spotted Deer, they all drove to Piccadilly Street, passed the Presbyterian Church on the corner, and found Mrs. Taylor's boarding house. It was a modest frame dwelling set in a half-acre garden in a quiet neighborhood. Mrs. Taylor was left a widow when her husband was killed in a fall from a runaway horse. Shortly afterward, she opened her house to rent rooms. She took people only through the recommendation of someone she knew. She and Carrie, a freed slave, ran a carefully managed home. Mrs. Taylor's boarding house soon became a favorite place for families to stay in Winchester.

## OLD CYRUS

That night, Robert went to Will Holliday's Tavern. The two men shared a drink, and Will began to inform Robert about some of the people he would be getting to know in Winchester.

"You'll meet Old Cyrus tomorrow morning. He's quite a character," Will said. "But he's a good man with a good heart. He'll be helping you and your family get settled on your land, so I imagine you'll get to know him quite well over the next few months."

"Does he have his own family?" asked Robert.

Will shook his head sadly. "Rachel, Old Cyrus's wife, died of typhoid fever while still a young woman. Cyrus was not at home when she died on a cold February morning. He had gone to find Dr. Foster, who came immediately to check on Rachel and to relieve my wife, Nancy, who had been sitting up all night with her. Once the doctor was on his way to his cottage, Cyrus went to milk his two cows and to gather some firewood. He was away a little more than an hour. When he returned to his cottage, Dr. Foster met him at the door and told him that his beloved Rachel was dead."

"What a sad tale," said Robert. "Has Cyrus married again?"

"No, he hasn't. Cyrus never forgave himself for not being with his wife when she was dying. Her death changed his life."

"But surely he must have found some way to go on?" asked Robert.

"Yes, and I'd like to think I helped in that a little. Shortly after Rachel's death, I asked Old Cyrus to take Spotted Deer, then just fourteen, as an apprentice. I noticed that Cyrus sat in front of my tavern seeking odd jobs. Cyrus's farm, except for his milk cows, looked rundown and neglected. With a young apprentice, Cyrus would have to find work in order to teach Spotted Deer a trade, so I asked him to take the lad and teach him carpentry. Together, they formed a good business, and Old Cyrus began to take an interest in his farm once again. Soon, Spotted Deer became Cyrus's adopted son, and both their lives took on a new meaning."

"Old Cyrus must get lonely without his wife," Robert mused, thinking of Sarah's unhappiness.

"Yes, but another friend came when he needed one most," Will replied, and went on to explain what he meant.

## WILL HOLLIDAY'S STORY

"On a morning in November, in the year of Rachel's death, a hawk circled the woods and settled into a large oak tree with a field mouse in his beak. Cyrus had gone out to his farm to milk the cows.

"Look," cried Spotted Deer to Cyrus, pointing to the bird of prey. "That hawk's enormous. Why does he keep circling?"

"There must be something else he's waiting to kill." Cyrus looked in the woods. By the stream, he found a hound puppy nearly frozen to death. Cyrus lifted the inert dog and carried him to his cabin. Inside, the remaining coals still glowed red on the hearth. Here Cyrus warmed the little dog and offered him some fresh cow's milk.

This puppy finally opened his dark eyes and looked at the old man, who now felt anxious for the dog's safety.

"Please get well, little one," Cyrus whispered. "I'll call you 'Daniel Morgan' after the greatest fightin' leader I've ever known."

The puppy licked the old man's hand and felt the fire warm before him.

"That's right," Old Cyrus encouraged, as he dipped his fingers in the warm milk and offered it to the puppy. "I fought with Daniel Morgan at the Battle of Cowpens in January of 1781, and with Light Horse Harry Lee and William Washington at Guilford Courthouse under General Nathanael Greene on March $15^{th}$ of the same year. Come on, little hound, those names should give you strength and double courage."

Old Cyrus rubbed the wet puppy dry and offered him more milk. "Drink it up, now, and with that name you'll be invincible."

The hawk finished his meal and circled the woods once more before he flew away. Spotted Deer watched him go, a large bird of prey gliding upon the air currents.

Cyrus always claimed that Rachel sent the little dog. After that day, he knew that his wife's spirit was with him. Spotted Deer felt that she was there, too, and she had used the hawk as her messenger.

"Daniel Morgan was mostly hound, and he had a deep hunting voice," Will continued. "With careful nursing, Cyrus brought the dog back to health, and the two of them became inseparable. Although Daniel Morgan was already the name of his horse, Cyrus couldn't resist the opportunity to name another noble creature after his brave fellow soldier in the War for Independence. So as not to confuse himself, he called the horse Dan and the dog Danny.

"Old Cyrus built a cabin on a piece of land just outside Winchester. Here, he and Danny enjoy their solitude. During the week, Cyrus lives in the cottage behind my tavern, but on weekends, he goes out to his farm with Danny and Spotted Deer."

Will Holliday explained that Spotted Deer milks the cows and takes care of the little farm while Old Cyrus finds customers for them. "It's a good business, and the Indian lad has learned his trade."

## THE LAND GRANT

The next morning, Spotted Deer arrived to take them to see the land grant, and with him in the wagon was an older man. "This is Cyrus," Spotted Deer said. "He's a good builder and can help you with the cabin."

Old Cyrus was of medium height and, though in his early sixties, he appeared strong and looked as if he had spent most of his life outdoors. He was clean-shaven and, although his hair was gray, it remained thick. He wore an old battered hat and smoked a corncob pipe. Mostly, he held it between his teeth and took it out to point the stem for emphasis when he was expressing an opinion.

Once they got settled into the wagon, Spotted Deer, Old Cyrus, and Robert headed westward toward the Allegheny Mountains.

"How long have you lived in Winchester?" Robert asked Old Cyrus.

"I came after the war because General Daniel Morgan lived here. Then I found Danny. He likes it here, and so do I," Cyrus explained.

"I hear that you tell a good tale, Cyrus," Robert remarked.

"And every word of it is true," Old Cyrus replied with great seriousness. "It all happened as I said. Danny likes Virginia's rabbits, and I didn't wish to try my luck again in North Carolina. It was too far to go; besides, Danny here may not like North Carolina rabbits."

"And the love of your life lived in Winchester," Spotted Deer added. "Tell the story as it really happened, Cyrus."

"I have two horses," Old Cyrus continued, ignoring Spotted Deer's comment. "This one is Dan, after General Daniel Morgan, with whom I fought at the Battle of Cowpens. And that lighter bay is Harry, after Light Horse Harry Lee. He fought at Guilford Courthouse. I was a lad of sixteen. I came down out of the North Carolina mountains with my friend, Sam, and my older brother, Joseph, to join General Morgan, as he was then on the South Carolina border. What a great fighter he was! None better for figuring out how to place troops and cavalry for a battle," Old Cyrus continued with enthusiasm.

"After that battle at Hannah's Cowpens, General Morgan couldn't ride a horse because of his piles. He turned his command over to General Greene. We headed north into Virginia, where Morgan left us. My brother and I went along with Nathaniel Greene and Lieutenant Colonel Harry Lee to Guilford Courthouse where we fought Cornwallis again." Cyrus then fell silent and blew on his corncob pipe. His dog, Danny, lay at his feet as the wagon continued toward the Allegheny Mountains.

The road they took was a well-used one, and suddenly, Robert's land lay before them. There were fields and a stream, and then several acres of woods. It was a real forest of oaks, maples, elms, and pines. Robert looked up in amazement. This landscape was something he had never seen in the valleys of Wales. He was used to seeing darkened villages and slag heaps from coal waste. Virginia was beautiful. Wales had the sea and castles and the Snowdonian Mountains.

"How wonderful!" Robert gasped. Cyrus brought the horses to a halt so that the three men could get a clearer view.

"Yes," replied Old Cyrus. "It is the goodliest land you'll ever find. There's even an old cabin here, which once belonged to a prospector who squatted by the stream some time ago."

Old Cyrus tethered his horses to a tree. Spotted Deer helped Robert climb out of the wagon, and they went to investigate the cabin.

Inside, cobwebs festooned the walls. They knocked down the cobwebs as they inspected the solidly built room.

It was a single room with a fireplace, some roughly made stools, a table, and a broken chimney constructed of unmortared stones.

"A poacher must have lived here recently," Spotted Deer said after he inspected the back of the cabin. "There's a set of traps hanging out there on a peg. The mud filler between the logs looks fairly new. He's not been gone long. I wonder why he didn't take his traps."

"He went off hunting and maybe he gave out before he could come back," Old Cyrus said. "Or maybe he got lost or went farther across the mountains. There's a gracious aplenty of wild game over to Tennessee. Anyway, he's a gone goosie, and it's our cabin now."

As Cyrus chatted, he poked about in the fireplace, examining the un-mortared flat stones and the solidness of the logs and mud filler.

Spotted Deer examined the floor, made of densely packed earth. He found the cabin's construction sound. The prospector had left recently, by the looks of the skins set to dry out back and flakes of tobacco scattered about the stone hearth. There was an odd-looking fishing rod behind the cabin with a dried worm still on the homemade hook. An old, torn shirt hung on a peg beside the door. Cyrus found three windows with glass in them.

"The prospector left and intended to return," Spotted Deer surmised. "Something changed his mind. I wonder what happened." He examined the ground and looked for tracks. "No, someone else came and must have met him. They left together," Spotted Deer concluded.

Old Cyrus didn't argue because he knew the Indian lad was probably right. Spotted Deer had a sixth sense about the ways of trappers and woodsmen.

Spotted Deer pointed out that much of the land grants were woods, but this land included open fields, too. "It's a good place," he told Robert. "The soil is fertile. The cabin will not take long to repair. What sort of farming are you planning to do?" He opened the cabin door, which hung on leather hinges with a stick put into a hasp to hold the door closed.

"I don't know," said Robert. "I've never farmed before. I've just mined coal."

"Well, you can use the fields for corn or for a market garden, and you'll need some chickens. You'll also want a cow and some pigs. General farming does well in this country," Old Cyrus explained.

"I hope I can get Sarah to like it. She wants to go back to Wales. She's not happy and knows little English. Luckily, we met some Welsh ladies on the wagon train, and there is a Welsh couple, Mr. and Mrs. Llewellyn, staying at Mrs. Taylor's boarding house with us."

"That's a nice place to stay," Cyrus assured him. "Just don't get in bad with Carrie. She's a terror if you bother her kitchen."

"I'll remember that," Robert said. He glanced at the cabin's fireplace. It was full of charred logs and looked cold and deserted.

"I understand she owns the kitchen, skillet, rolling pin, and all," added Spotted Deer.

"Carrie's all right, but she's the boss, that's for sure," said Old Cyrus. "She takes nothing off anyone. Carrie had been a slave in the Taylor family since she was a child, but now she's a freed slave. Mr. Taylor freed Carrie and her husband so they could stay together. She's been at the boarding house since Mrs. Taylor first opened it. Everyone knows to obey Carrie because she runs that place with an iron hand. She has two nice boys, Zack and Tommy, who run errands for her. I often go by and tell them stories of our War for Independence and of the battles I fought."

The men examined the room again. They found odd bits of furniture, an old iron pot, and little more. "I think it's soundly built," Old Cyrus remarked. "We'll have to clean it up a bit and put more mud fill between the logs. We need to reset the unmortared stones in the chimney, too. You're lucky to have the stream to provide clean mountain water for your family and the livestock. It'll also allow for irrigation. This is an ideal piece of property."

Old Cyrus not only understood building, but also how to reuse materials. He knew the other carpenters and stonemasons in Winchester and bargained with them for supplies. Cyrus and Spotted Deer were experts in acquiring the best materials. Robert was in good hands.

"How long do you think it will take to fix up the cabin?" Robert asked, as the men continued to survey the building.

"I'd say a month or so. Since we have a structure to start with, it'll be easier. It's not much of a place, but it's a beginning," Cyrus answered, as he thumped the cabin's wood to test its soundness.

Robert agreed. Old Cyrus and Spotted Deer decided to begin work immediately. It was the beginning of August, so the good weather would last three more months.

## THE CABIN

Later that week, Old Cyrus and Spotted Deer again brought Robert, this time with his daughters, out to the farm. They planned to work on the cabin and to clear the area around it of weeds and undergrowth.

Before the group left Mrs. Taylor's house that morning, Carrie packed a picnic lunch. "I'm sending Zack and Tommy to help you with this picnic," she told Annie. "There are old pieces of torn rug that will do to sit on. They also know the snakes and spiders to stay clear of. Don't touch a rattlesnake or a copperhead—they'll kill you. Also, black widow spiders—you want no truck with them either. There're a lot of creepy-crawlies in the mountains. Take my advice and whitewash that cabin before you open your lunch hamper."

With those words, Carrie saw the girls and her sons into the wagon. Sarah decided she did not feel well and wished to stay at the boarding house.

Old Cyrus picked up the reins as Spotted Deer took Light Horse Harry's bridle and led him and Daniel Morgan down the driveway onto Piccadilly Street.

"I guess we've got our marching orders," the Indian lad told Old Cyrus as he checked the horses' harness and tightened a trace before he also climbed onto the wagon. Spotted Deer sat on the hard seat next to Old Cyrus. They turned westward and soon left Winchester.

"It'll take us about an hour to reach the land grant," Old Cyrus said to the boys, as Robert and his daughters settled into the wagon.

Zack and Tommy sat at the back and cradled themselves on two sacks filled with pieces of old carpet to sit on for the picnic. They also carried tools, strong soap, and some rags for cleaning the cabin. Zack guarded the lunch in the hamper from Danny, who sniffed it inquisitively. Cyrus had contributed some homemade beer and a jug of moonshine, which he kept under the seat of his wagon so it was handy if he wanted a drink.

"Can you tell us some stories?" Tommy encouraged Old Cyrus. "About the war and Daniel Morgan? The general, not your horse or dog."

That little encouragement was all Cyrus needed to begin his favorite tale.

"When I lived in Buncombe County near the French Broad River, on my father's farm, news of the British Major Patrick Ferguson's defeat at King's Mountain soon reached us. John Miller, a neighbor of ours, came home limping. He fought there with the patriots' militia under Colonel Isaac Shelby and was wounded. 'Twernt serious, so he dressed it with moonshine to keep the infection out. He also dressed it with British rum, since he didn't care to drink it. Too sweet. It's made from molasses. Not my taste, either." Old Cyrus stuffed tobacco into his unlit pipe and put it back in his mouth. "He'd used it on a snake bite from a bell tail and knowed hit worked, once he'd sucked the poison out after cutting his hand with his knife where the snake bit him.

"My older brother, Joseph, was eighteen, and he wanted to go down to the South Carolina border and join the militia under General Daniel Morgan. That inspired my friend, Sam, and me to go with him. We were just sixteen, but we knowed how to shoot our Kentucky rifles, and we both were accurate at hitting game. We each rode a half-broken pony that was too wild and too light for farm work. We didn't tell my pa that we were going, but I told my sister, Mary, who was older than Joseph. She had good sense and knowed how to break the news to our pa. We made her promise not to tell a livin' soul until we got a long ways off from home.

"So we rode down out of the mountains and met other young men and boys. Some were mounted on horses, some thumbed a lift on farm wagons, and others walked.

We all wanted to join General Daniel Morgan, who was known as a great fighter in the French and Indian War with General George Washington. Morgan even fought in Canada against the French.

"General Morgan was called the 'Old Wagoner' because he took care of the supply wagons and brought them safely to George Washington. Morgan took a bullet at the back of his neck. Hit knocked out his teeth in the left jaw, and that bullet came right through his cheek. He had the most wonderfulest scar! I'd never see'd anything like hit, and Morgan still standing up alive to tell you about hit!"

"When did this happen?" Spotted Deer asked Cyrus.

"I reckon hit was 1757 or '59, somethin' like that. Hit was quite near Winchester at the Hanging Rock."

"Tell us more about the war, Cyrus!" Tommy exclaimed, hoping for an exciting story.

"In 1780, the patriots had almost lost the war in the South," Cyrus began again, setting the scene for his listeners. "Charleston and Savannah had fallen to the British commander, Lord General Cornwallis, who had defeated Colonel Buford and his men at Camden, South Carolina. Into this grave situation, George Washington sent a northern Quaker, General Nathanael Greene, who put his pacification aside to defend his country. He was to replace General Gates, who was making a hash of things in North and South Carolina.

"In three and a half months, General Greene built a winning strategy in an unusual way and wore down General Cornwallis and his well-equipped army. General Greene allowed the British to go east to Wilmington, North Carolina, and eventually they became trapped at Gloucester Point across the river from Yorktown, where General Cornwallis surrendered—only he was sick and his second-in-command did it for him. So much for gallantry!

"George Washington sent General Greene to

Charlotte as the Commander of the Southern Forces, and Greene was told to study the streams and many rivers that crisscross the Carolinas' swampy, pine-tree-covered land. The pines are tall and their trunks are dark, especially after a rain, and the pine barrens look kind of spooky, particularly to foreigners who don't know our North Carolina swamps. Some of the British prisoners found them scary, like sentinels guarding rivers and fords. The pine barrens made great places to hide when we ambushed Colonel "Benny" Tarleton's Legion.

"The British fought in a line, but we hid behind trees and rocks to pick off the silly beggars! Don't they understand Indian-style fighting? You'd think they were fighting Napoleon, all dressed up with bagpipes and drums in those plaid skirts. I never see'd so many knobby knees. Kilts, those skirts are called, and they weigh almost as much as a young sheep when dry. Wet, they would drown you crossing a ford! No wonder so many soldiers drowned at Cowan's Ford. Hit weren't bullets that killed some of the Scots, but those sodden kilts and their fifty-pound backpacks and the eight-pound guns they carried. Those heavy wet tartans and the current and the everlasting rain is what killed 'em.

"You never see'd the amount of rain we slogged in to reach Sherrild's Ford. The red clay about tore up our boots, and our clothes were in shreds. Some of us had only blankets we wrapped around ourselves like Indians. The wagons got stuck, and three horses went down trying to pull the wheels out of the deep clay where they'd sunk.

"How we ever met up with General Greene's forces at Guilford Courthouse and made it to the River Dan, I'll never know. Daniel Morgan's 'Flying Army' did, though, and we got into Virginia before Benny Tarleton and Lord General Cornwallis ever made it. That General Morgan was as smart as a tree full of owls. The militia was filled by men who'd growed up knowing the pine barrens and the fords.

They fished in the many streams, and had crossed and recrossed the Catawba and the Yadkin Rivers and knowed the way. General Greene had a map drawn up with the help of the men who knew such things, and soon he understood the land and its many creeks and rivers as well as those who were born on them. Lord General Cornwallis did not study the land, and he came up from Cowpens long after Morgan had crossed the Catawba River and was on his way to the River Dan and Virginia.

"General Morgan reached Sherrild's Ford on the 30$^{th}$ of January. Morgan wanted to go west toward the mountains, but General Greene decided to go north into Virginia where he could resupply his army. 'He's ours,' Greene told us, but we all wondered how. General Greene was a sly bird, however, with a lot of sense. 'We must be chased northward, but not caught,' Greene told Morgan. 'That way, we can resupply the men and get fresh horses and meet the British generals at a battlefield of my own choosing. Now we'll go on before Cornwallis can get his troops across the Catawba. We'll leave General William Davidson and his five hundred-man militia to harass the enemy crossing at Cowan's Ford.'

"The British were led by two Irishmen, Charles O'Hara and Alexander Leslie. They were foolish because they abandoned their wagons and their supplies. At Cowan's Ford, O'Hara's horse fell and Lord General Cornwallis's horse was shot, but made it across the river. Then it dropped dead. The troops were up to their chests in the January-cold river water, with a rapid current. Such a mess! But Morgan and General Greene were clear of the Catawba River on their way to cross the Dan into Virginia. Once there, they would get us fresh horses and supplies.

"We found that von Steuben had trained militia at Jenning's Ordinary, and wonderfulest of all, we found shoes and uniforms. My feet were red with the cold, and my torn footwear was leaking—the leather was in tatters.

Once north of the Dan, we found horses, fodder, ammonition, fresh troops, and plenty of food in Virginia." Old Cyrus paused in his story to take a breath. "I reckon that's enough of a tale for today, boys," he said, after a minute. "After all, I've got to save some stories for later."

The group rode along quietly toward the land grant for what seemed like a long time.

"How many years have you lived here, Cyrus?" asked Robert, finally, breaking the silence.

"I came after the war because General Daniel Morgan lived in Winchester. Since my elder brother, Joseph, inherited the home place in North Carolina, I decided to move along and came up the Great Wagon Road to Virginia.

"My wife Rachel and I got married a year or so later. That made a difference." Old Cyrus coughed suddenly and appeared to choke. When he stopped coughing, Annie saw tears in his eyes. Spotted Deer took the reins and drove the horses while Cyrus recovered himself.

Quietly, Annie passed her freshly washed white handkerchief to Cyrus. He nodded his thank-you and brushed the tears from his cheeks. Annie realized the memory of his deceased wife remained very painful.

"Danny likes it here," Old Cyrus explained, as he blew his nose and drew in a deep breath. "Will Holliday lets me stay in his cabin behind his Tavern. I have a small farm not far from there, so Spotted Deer and I can keep our eye on it. We have steady employment doing carpentry work and odd jobs."

"It wasn't your dog who kept you here. It was Rachel who wanted you to live in Virginia," Spotted Deer reminded him

"That, too," Old Cyrus agreed. "But that's another story."

"She was the main story for a while," Spotted Deer

said.

"Yes, but Rachel died and I couldn't leave. My dog, Danny, came later, and he likes it here. When I see a hawk or a great bird flying free, I know that Rachel's spirit is here. I couldn't leave her and return to my first home in North Carolina. She might not know where I'd moved to, and I'd lose her again."

Old Cyrus allowed the horses more rein as they drew the wagon up a rocky incline on the road, which led to the Allegheny Mountains. Spotted Deer got out of the heavily loaded wagon and led the horses up a difficult hill.

When they finally arrived at the land grant, Annie and Ellen scrubbed the walls until they were free of cobwebs and dust. Robert and Spotted Deer cleared the undergrowth and cut a path beside the stream through to the site of the proposed barn.

Old Cyrus dug a shallow trench to show the outline of the future barn. He also cleared away the branches that had fallen during a recent thunderstorm and obstructed the road.

## ZACK AND TOMMY

Carrie had two children, Zack and Tommy. Soon after arriving in Winchester, Mrs. Glynis and Miss Gwynn began to teach the two boys. Mrs. Glynis taught both of them to read, and Miss Gwynn taught Tommy to play the piano.

It was not legal to set slaves free in Tidewater Virginia, but freed slaves were recognized in the Shenandoah Valley. In most of the south, it was illegal to teach a Negro child to read and write. Although Mr. Taylor bought Carrie's husband and had papers on him, the concept of a slave being free was a new idea. It was illegal for Mrs. Glynis and Miss Gwynn to teach Zack and Tommy, but being Welsh, they didn't know Virginia's laws.

With its large German and Scots-Irish population, the valley did not use a lot of slave labor, and the execution of the law was more lenient. Mrs. Taylor still warned Mrs. Glynis and Miss Gwynn not to mention that they were teaching two Negro children.

"Be careful," she said to the Welsh ladies. "Carrie is delighted that her boys are learning. Tommy loves to play the piano, and Zack is a quick learner—he's already reading the books I have in my library. But this arrangement could cause you a lot of trouble."

"I shall be careful," Mrs. Glynis had promised. "But who heard of a law that is enforced in one part of Virginia and is not applicable in another? Why is the entire state not the same?"

"I don't know," Mrs. Taylor replied. "Just keep quiet, and don't mention that you're teaching Carrie's boys. That's our secret."

The boys felt proud that they could read, and Tommy played the piano almost like a professional. He could make his living in music if he got the chance.

Zack was a curious child, full of questions for Mrs. Glynis. Once, they spent a whole afternoon talking about navigation. Zack wanted to know about time and the movement of the ships.

"How do the ships' captains know where they are going when they cross the ocean?" he questioned Mrs. Glynis.

She told him the amount of time it had taken her to get from Wales to Philadelphia. "The boat left Liverpool at a high tide in England. It is five hours earlier in America. So when the boat left early in the morning in England, it was still the middle of the night in Philadelphia."

Zack looked puzzled. "You mean that when it's morning in Wales, it's still nighttime in America?"

"Yes, that's right," Mrs. Glynis told him. "The sun travels westward from Australia and China. It crosses Europe and ends up at last in America."

"So if I have supper in the evening, the children in Wales would be in bed?" Tommy wanted to know.

"That's right," Mrs. Glynis said. "It would be much later in the evening in Wales and in London. That's called longitude. Latitude is distance."

"Columbus must have been a marvelous navigator and a very smart man to understand all of that!" Zack exclaimed. "He really must have taken a great chance to come to America. What if he had ended up in Australia instead?"

"Captain Cook discovered the eastern side of Australia and the Great Barrier Reef," Mrs. Glynis told them. "But later, not in 1492. By Captain Cook's day, navigation had progressed. Cook was the first captain to use navigation as a science. He also increased our knowledge of world geography."

Zack listened, wide-eyed, and absorbed as much information as he could. He and Tommy both loved afternoons with Mrs. Glynis.

"Captain Cook was killed in Hawaii in 1779 by the people who lived there. He was fifty and he gave us a lot of information about the St. Lawrence River and the islands in the Pacific Ocean," Mrs. Glynis told him, and she loaned him a book and a map to show Zack where Cook's voyages took him.

## OLD CYRUS' TALES

"Did I ever tell you about why they call the North Carolinians 'Tar Heels'?" Old Cyrus asked Zack and Tommy as they sat on the back steps of Mrs. Taylor's house one warm September evening. Cyrus was in Winchester to get supplies and planned to stay the night at his old cabin behind Will Holliday's Tavern, then drive back to the farm the next morning. Carrie made them a hot supper, and the two boys and Old Cyrus felt happy to possess full stomachs and some good storytelling company.

"No, Mr. Cyrus, you haven't. You can tell some wonderful tales, but are they about things that really happened?" Zack wanted to know as the boys settled comfortably on the steps.

The old man pretended to look hurt. "Upon my honor." He put up his hand as if to take an oath. "Every word I'm telling you is the truth."

"Well, go on," Tommy replied, eager to hear the story. "I don't care if it's true or not. It sounds like a mighty fine tale."

"I didn't fight at King's Mountain, but I had a cousin, James, who did. What a battle that was! First of all, Major Ferguson and his regulars took the mountain. The rest of his troops were Loyalist militia from the border of North and South Carolina. They remained loyal to King George and fought with the British. The Patriots were under Colonel Isaac Shelby and Colonel William Campbell. They surrounded the mountain and fought Indian-style. Their Kentucky long rifles defeated Major Ferguson, who died in the battle.

"Reverend Sam Doak offered spiritual guidance and told the Patriots to shout this battle cry, 'The Sword of the Lord and Gideon,' just like in Biblical days. The battle lasted just over an hour, and Campbell's men dug in and fought Indian-style, hiding behind trees and thickets and rocks. They became almost invisible with their linsey-woolsey clothes. The Loyalists were encircled, but the shooting continued. The Patriots disregarded the white flags because they wanted to reap revenge on Lieutenant Colonel Tarleton, who killed his prisoners. They called him 'Butcher,' and that he was.

"In the thick of the battle, some troops under one of the Patriot commanders began to fall back, whereupon their officers shouted, 'Stand firm like the North Carolinians, who have tar on their heels.' That," proclaimed Old Cyrus, "is how we got our nickname. You'll hear other stories about getting tar on your feet crossing the Tar River, but don't take no notice of them tales. My cousin James fought at King's Mountain, and he knows what happened."

"Tell us another one of your tales, Mr. Cyrus," begged Tommy.

"And make sure it's another true one," added Zack.

"Of course it'll be a true one!" Cyrus exclaimed, turning red in the face. "All of my stories are true." He regained his composure. "Let's see. During the War of Independence, we had a difficult time getting supplies, so we made locust beer from the pods of locust trees. I kept it in a powder horn flask in my boot. The beer wasn't strong, but it was a refreshing drink after all the work we did fighting the British." He stopped to light his pipe.

"Then, in a second powder horn flask, we kept moonshine or corn whiskey. The British preferred the rum they got from Jamaica, but I ain't ever took to it. Rum's made from molasses, which is made from sugar cane. They had a lot of sugar cane in the Virgin Islands.

"Corn whiskey was a handy thing to have because we could swap it for food, a warm blanket, and even ammo-nition. Since I growed up in the North Carolina mountains, I was well acquainted with the finer secrets of good corn whiskey. My brother, Joseph, and I kept our North Carolina Company well supplied before the Battle of

Cowpens.

"When Nathaneal Greene took over the army in the south from General Gates, General George Washington told his new commander to study the rivers and the streams which crisscrossed the states of North and South Carolina. General Greene sent one of his colonels and his men out to survey the land and to draw a map of North Carolina's rivers and many creeks. At the finish, General Greene knowed more about the rivers and swamps of the Carolinas than even the natives who had growed up there and fished in those streams. Unlike Virginia, with its majestic James and Rappahannock Rivers, the river system in North and South Carolina is not dependent upon a few big rivers, but on many smaller ones which crisscross the Carolinas and make the land swampy. Lord General Cornwallis had little knowledge of our river system, and that led to his defeat—that and his lack of tactics. He just bursted through with his troops without any thought of the lay of the land or depth of the rivers that ran through it. 'Benny' Tarleton was the same—run and hack and run some more.

"Now, Daniel Morgan took careful study of the land, the hills, the undergrowth, and the way the troops could leave the battlefield without getting caught between rivers or in thick undergrowth. Morgan and General Greene took all that into account, and that's why we won the Battle of Cowpens in fifty minutes," Old Cyrus explained. "Morgan understood the topography.

"After Cowpens, Morgan and Colonel William Washington raced north toward Virginia to resupply their troops with fresh horses, food, and even clothing. The skies opened up and the pine barrens of North Carolina soon became a sea of red clay mud.

"General Greene took his ill-fed, poorly clothed, and partly trained troops and raced for the Dan River, which marked the border of Virginia. He wanted to reach the river first, cross over it, and pull the boats onto the northern side to prevent the British from crossing.

"It was important to keep the two armies divided because, if the British had crossed the Dan River into Virginia, they would have probably intercepted Thomas Jefferson and the other leaders traveling near Charlottesville and arrested them. Then the British would have had a clear march to Richmond, and we would have been defeated. We met General Greene's forces near Salisbury, and the two Patriot armies linked up. We raced northward in endless rain. We raced to the Dan River and got there first. General Greene had bateaux constructed when he first took over the command, and we carried the boats with us.

"Later, after the Battle of Guilford Courthouse, Nathaneal Greene headed south into the other Carolina. Greene was from a Quaker family, and General Washington had sent him from Pennsylvania. We linked up with Francis Marion, whom the British called the 'Swamp Fox,' and irascible ole 'Gamecock' Sumter. I even found a still near Eutaw Springs, where we fought a mighty battle. You could say, from my point of view, that the War of Independence was won on the colonists' supply of corn whiskey. Lord General Cornwallis and Banastre Tarleton never understood the vital importance of American moonshine! It has no comparison for refreshment to their terrible-tasting rum."

"Where in the mountains did you grow up, Mr. Cyrus?" Tommy asked. "Where did your family live?"

"In Buncombe County. My daddy had a farm up there. He and Mama raised eight children. Joseph was the eldest. He was eighteen when we came down together from the mountains to fight in the war against the British. I was sixteen. My friend, Sam, who came with us, was also sixteen. We were looking for adventure, and we were powerful shots with a gun. I still am." Old Cyrus assured them he could shoot game as well as any man half his age.

"Mama and Daddy raised five boys and three girls. With two of us gone to fight the British, that left the three younger boys to help on the farm: John, Roy, and Michael."

There was a brief silence while the three of them sat under the oak trees that warm autumn evening, enjoying each other's company. Danny, the brown and white hound, whom Cyrus claimed his wife sent to him after she died, got up and stretched his cramped limbs before he lay back down under the porch to get away from the mosquitoes. Cyrus lit his pipe to smoke out the mosquitoes. "The smoke chases them away. You drown them in smoke and they won't bite you," he explained. As the boys watched, the old man drew in on the tobacco in his pipe in order to keep it lit.

Then Cyrus abruptly changed the subject. "I hear you are learning to read," he said. "Is it easy?"

"Reading's not too hard," Zack replied. "I'm getting the sense of it."

"One time I could read, but I forgot how. I can write my name and Joseph could, too," Cyrus said, proud of this accomplishment. "A fellow in my company taught some of his troops to read because we needed to know how to look after our Brown Bess muskets. I can still write, but since I ain't studyin' reading, I forget."

"Who was Brown Bess?" Tommy asked, curious about the name.

"It's a musket named after Queen Elizabeth, who lived a long time ago. To honor her, the English named the gun after their queen," Old Cyrus answered, shaking his head. "I can't see why that was such an honor, since the ball was a large as a marble, and it'd put a hole in you big enough for a mouse to creep through. We had Kentucky rifles, which had a much longer range and were accurate up to 300 yards. We captured a few muskets and used them, too. The British were testing breech-loading rifles at the

Battle of Saratoga."

"Reading is not too hard if you know the letters, Mr. Cyrus. It shouldn't be hard to learn the sounds," Tommy assured him. "Then you put the letters and sounds together and make words."

Old Cyrus changed the subject. "The sun's taking his leave of us for today. Hit'll be dark soon, and the lightning bugs will come out and light their lanterns. The cicadas will sing, and old Mr. Tree Toad will croak his evening song. They'll serenade the tired sun to his rest."

"Where does the sun go?" Tommy asked. "Does it sleep, too?"

"No, it shines in India and China," Zack explained. "Then in the morning it comes back to shine on us."

"Who told you that?" Old Cyrus asked. He didn't believe Zack, and blew pipe smoke in a great cloud to keep off the mosquitoes.

"Mrs. Glynis and Miss Gwynn know about such things. People from Wales are mighty smart," answered Zack, eager to defend his teachers. "They came to America on a big ship, and the time in Wales is five hours ahead of us because the sun gets to Wales first. It travels west, and Wales is east of us. Some scientist figured it out, and the ships' captains know about it because of navigation."

"Well, I never heard of such a thing," Old Cyrus exclained. "How do you know that's true?"

"The ships' captains tell you about the sun's time in different places. How do you think Columbus found America if he didn't know about the times getting there?"

"We ain't got no ships' captains in Winchester. We're two hundred miles away from places like Yorktown, and even more hundreds from Charlestown. I was in Charlestown in the war, and the time there was just the same," Cyrus told them. "Francis Marion kept everyone on time. There was no Welsh time about him."

Zack and Tommy sat a while longer on the steps

and watched the shadows deepen. The lightning bugs came out and flashed their tiny lights. The mosquitoes started to bite. Although Old Cyrus sent up clouds of smoke, the bugs did not go away.

"Well, that's my bag of stories for tonight. I best be going," Cyrus told the boys. "I'm a-stayin in town, as Robert and Spotted Deer are in the mountains to take care of the farm. I told Will Holliday I'd do some work for him tomorrow."

Old Cyrus gave a soft whistle, and Danny appeared from under the steps and pricked up his ears in anticipation of leaving Mrs. Taylor's house and returning to their cabin behind Will Holliday's Tavern. Cyrus's pipe made a red glow as he walked down the street with Danny at his heels.

"Come on, Zack," said Tommy. "Let's go inside. In spite of Mr. Cyrus's pipe smoke, I'm bites all over. Mama will call us soon to come in."

Zack lingered for a minute in thought. "I didn't realize how important moonshine whiskey was in winning our War of Independence."

"According to Mr. Cyrus, the colonists would have lost without it," Tommy replied as the brothers entered the house.

## SARAH'S TRIP TO THE MARKET

After a month of steady work, Robert was ready to bring Sarah and the girls out to see their new homestead. "I'm sure your wife will like it," Old Cyrus encouraged Robert. "It's as nice as you could get."

"It's a good, tight cabin," Spotted Deer agreed. "Anyone would like it."

"Sarah still wants to return to Wales, where she can speak her own language," Robert explained. "She is not happy in America." The three men sat by the kitchen fire and chatted while Old Cyrus smoked his pipe. Danny lay at his feet and whimpered in his dreams.

"I'll try to convince Sarah that Virginia has its good points, too," Old Cyrus said. "You can't find anything better where weather is concerned. It's a good house we've built. Anyone would be proud to own it. Now what you need is to buy some pigs. This is apple-growing country, so a few trees would do just fine. I think it is a great homestead, if you ask me." Old Cyrus felt satisfied with the farmhouse. "My pipe's gone out. I think I need a new one that will stay lit." He emptied the pipe's cold tobacco into the fire.

"Even so, I hope Sarah will appreciate it," Robert replied. "The girls don't worry me, but I fear that Sarah will never get used to living in Virginia."

Later that evening, back at Mrs. Taylor's boarding house, Robert described the cabin to his wife and daughters. "It's a mixed one hundred acres, with woods and fields," he told them. "The cabin is sound, and I have spring water up near the house. When do you plan to move out with me?"

"It sounds nice, but I prefer to go back to Wales," Sarah said. "It's all so strange here."

"Papa says he'll take you out to see the cabin for your inspection," Ellen told her mother.

Sarah burst into tears. "I don't want to live all alone in the country, miles away from everyone I know! I like it here at Mrs. Taylor's house. There is company, and I am learning English. Carrie makes me tea, and we talk."

Robert felt deeply hurt by Sarah's outburst. Yorweth took his arm and the two men went to Will Holliday's Tavern, leaving Sarah with the women. Robert didn't know what to say to his wife, so he sought the company of men.

Meanwhile Annie pleaded, "Mother, just go and see the farm. It is beautiful, and Father has worked doubly hard to have it all done before it gets cold. There are mountains and trees and a clear stream."

"I never wanted to come to America in the first place," sobbed Sarah. "I never wanted to leave Wales. I never wanted to have a farm. I'm being forced into it."

Annie got up and left the room. She had heard these complaints numerous times. She knocked quietly on the kitchen door and asked Carrie if she had a moment to talk.

Carrie invited Annie into her well-ordered kitchen. "Come and sit down, and I will make you a cup of tea." She took down Granny Jones's teapot.

"I don't know what to do, Carrie," Annie cried. "It's impossible to get Mother interested in the farm. Papa has worked so hard and has tried to please her, but Mother simply won't cooperate. Ellen is just as worried as I am."

Annie sat at the kitchen table and dried her eyes. "Suppose Mother never settles?" she asked Carrie. "Suppose she never goes to live at the farm? Then what can we do?"

Carrie didn't know what to say. The Jones family had sailed across an ocean, and they had spent almost three weeks on a wagon train to come to Winchester. Everyone hoped Sarah would feel happier once she had a home in America. Now Annie felt it was all in vain. Her mother refused to take part in American life; all she did was sit at

Mrs. Taylor's house and cry.

Annie at first was hopeful that once they got the farm, her mother would try to like their new home, but nothing they said changed Sarah's overwhelming feeling of homesickness.

"We can never go home," Sarah told her daughters over and over. "I'll never see Wales again."

During these times, Ellen usually left the room to escape her mother's sadness. Annie tried to interest her in the pretty town of Winchester. They spent time visiting the shops, and occasionally Old Cyrus drove them to the farmers' market.

A few weeks after Annie's talk with Carrie in the kitchen, Charlie arrived unexpectedly at Mrs. Taylor's boarding house with his wagon and team. It was a beautiful Saturday morning in September.

Ellen had come down with a cold that weekend and wasn't up to seeing visitors, so Carrie called Annie and Sarah downstairs.

"Hello, Annie! Hello Sarah," Charlie greeted them.

Annie smiled, but Sarah looked grim. "Good morning, Charlie," she said. "What brings you to Winchester?"

"Can I take you ladies out for a drive with Jefferson and Madison?" Charlie inquired.

"That would be a treat!" exclaimed Annie, delighted to see their old friend. Before Sarah could complain, Annie bundled her out and into the wagon.

"You came all this way just to go to the farmers' market?" Annie asked Charlie as they drove along to the outskirts of Winchester.

"I wanted to see you ladies," Charlie explained. "And to ask a friend here about swapping him some Patton cattle for a fine shorthorn bull he's got." He drove the wagon down Piccadilly Street onto Boscowan.

"How is Mrs. Charlie?" Annie asked. "And James,

your son?"

"They send their compliments and hope to meet you soon," Charlie replied as they pulled into the farmers' market and tethered the horses under the trees among the farm wagons and carriages.

"The apples should be coming in now," Charlie remarked. "Sarah, you'll love that wonderful fruit."

"Yes, Carrie gave us some applies only yesterday and told us the story of Johnny Appleseed, the man who planted apple trees," Sarah replied.

"Yes, he's quite a character." Charlie laughed as he helped Sarah down from the wagon. "Now let's go and see what's in the market today."

Sarah's attention was diverted from her homesickness while they wandered through the covered market. Annie found patchwork quilts, Shenandoah Valley oak baskets, and woven goods among the fruits and vegetables.

"Look at the sweet corn and pumpkins!" Charlie said excitedly. "The market is bustling with customers and vendors." He stopped at every stall to ask questions about the food and handicrafts.

Sarah was impressed by the array of fruits and vegetables and the fresh eggs and honey. "Autumn in the Shenandoah Valley is indeed a bountiful time," she admitted.

"Try my apples," one vendor said, handing a slice to Sarah. "Very good, eh?"

Sarah ate samples of each farmer's wares until she felt stuffed with good food. For an hour, she became happy and animated. Annie guided her mother through the market, both of them eager to try new things.

"Come," said Charlie. "We'd best be on our way. Jefferson will be restive, and he can cause trouble."

Charlie guided Sarah and Annie back to the lot under the trees that was reserved for horses and wagons.

Here, they found a sleepy Madison and Jefferson, whisking flies from their backs with lazy tails. They appeared quite happy and content.

Charlie helped Sarah into the wagon. Annie followed her mother, and they sat in the seat as Charlie untied the horses and picked up the reins. Then he climbed up beside the women and drove them home.

"That was fun!" Annie exclaimed as they headed toward Mrs. Taylor's house. "I'm glad you came to see us."

"Yes," agreed Sarah. "I've never seen so many different kinds of food in one place. Thank you, Charlie. What a nice day you've given us."

## COUNTRY MATTERS

Another time, Charlie came up from New Town to take Robert to visit Yorweth and Blodwen on their farm. The farm was three miles east of Robert's land and not as well laid out. With the help of a local lad, Peter Wilson, Yorweth built a small I-house and began to stock the farm with milk cows and six Leicester Longwool sheep.

"I have found a loom for you," Yorweth told his wife. "Charlie is coming up to help move it out here. It's a German-made loom, but very much like our Welsh ones. Robert asked Spotted Deer to come and help us set it up."

Out at the back of the I-house was a one-story ell, which is typical of the I-house style. Here were the workrooms, and here Blodwen would set up her loom and store her wool. She told some of the members of her church that she hoped to become a weaver.

She and Yorweth attended the Methodist Church in Winchester, where she met other Welsh immigrants who also owned farms. It was here they met a lively young couple, Thomas Harris and his wife, Ariel, who helped supply the linen flax and the wool she needed.

"That's an unusual name," Blodwen told her new friend one morning when they met for a chat and a hot drink after church.

"I was named for Ariel in *The Tempest*. My father was an admirer of Shakespeare," Ariel explained. "He loved *The Tempest* in particular and could quote long passages from it. When I was born, he named me Ariel over my mother's protests. He went to London to join an acting troup after my mother died."

The little Methodist church was blessed with an active congregation and was filled with lively young people. When Charlie came to visit the stock sales, he often stayed with Yorweth and Blodwen. Their home was less crowded than Robert's house, with Old Cyrus, Spotted

Deer, and the two dogs all snoring in unison and shaking the rafters of the cabin after a long day's work.

"You'll get no sleep here with our snoring concert," Old Cyrus warned Charlie. "You're welcome, but you might not want to stay."

Charlie advised Yorweth on how to buy livestock, and Yorweth introduced him to Leicester Longwool sheep.

"Look at those sheep!" Charlie cried. "They look like nothing I've ever seen before."

"They have wonderful pelts, and their wool is long and curling. It's great for weaving cloth. Tell Robert to get some of those sheep, because the German weavers will love them. The pelts can weigh as much as 75 pounds and will bring a good profit," Yorweth explained to Charlie. "With the part-linen and part-wool linsey-woolsey clothing people wear here, these sheep will become a bonus."

Yorweth showed Charlie his small flock, which he let out of the barn. "The only problem is they are hard to herd and object to dogs," he said. "The rams are fairly large and are naturally polled, so you don't have to worry about horns. Once they settle down, they are good keepers."

"Old Cyrus will love them," Charlie said. "Though if these sheep can't be herded, they'll cause him endless trouble. He'll have a million stories about chasing rams and about his dogs' dizzy-headedness trying to catch up with them."

Yorweth laughed, and the two men went to look at the enclosed ell, where they planned to put the new loom.

## OLD CYRUS NAMES THE LEICESTER RAMS

Old Cyrus stood at the pasture fence as Charlie and Robert unloaded two Leicester Longwool rams from the farm wagon. The sheep each weighed about 250 pounds and had long, curling fleece. They came from the livestock sale that morning in Winchester.

"Those are big, upstanding rams," Cyrus remarked as Charlie and Robert freed them from their crates. Charlie came and joined Old Cyrus at the fence while Robert put the sheep in the horse's stalls in the newly finished barn and swept down the wagon.

"The Leicester sheep were imported from England right after the War of Independence because the Scots-Irish preferred them for their long wool. The Scots and the Irish are great weavers, and they have kept their home looms to make clothes out of wool and linen. That's why we grow so much flax—it's for the linen fibers," Charlie explained. "These rams can be unpredictable, though, because they don't like herding dogs."

"Monty will soon fix that," Old Cyrus assured him, lighting his pipe. "He's already shown he takes no saucy stuff when it comes to herding the ewes. They'll soon know who's boss, even if they have to walk backwards all the way to the barn." Old Cyrus relit his corncob pipe after his first attempt failed.

Robert was thankful Charlie had brought Monty to the farm. He could already herd ewes and would soon manage the rams.

Charlie and Robert freed the rams from their stalls and led them into the pasture. Cyrus swung open the gate to allow the sheep to go through and promptly closed it behind them.

Monty watched with interest as the rams were turned loose to roam and to graze where they pleased.

"Not bad-looking animals," observed Old Cyrus as

he pulled on his pipe. "We should get some good young-uns in the spring."

The rams eyed the curious dog with suspicion. They turned to face Monty, who tried to direct them to the far end of the field where the stream ran through the pasture. Monty stood his ground, and the rams held theirs. Finally, Monty lay down and the rams relaxed and nibbled at the grass. When Monty sat up, the rams raised their heads.

"Silly old sheep," Cyrus said aloud. "Don't they know Monty always gets his way?"

"These are good rams," Charlie replied when he joined Old Cyrus at the gate. "They'll upgrade the original stock."

Robert drove the horses into the upper barn to unhitch them from the wagon and to rub them down.

Old Cyrus pulled out his almost-lit pipe and knocked out the ash against the gate. He knew that Robert objected to anyone smoking around the farm buildings filled with hay and grain. A spark from the pipe could easily set off a fire, and Cyrus respected his friend's wishes.

"Those rams got a mind of their own," Old Cyrus said, as he placed his pipe in his pocket. "They could cause us a lot of trouble. But they look like grand, big animals—they're naturally polled with no horns to knock down fences or injure other stock, and they're petti-greed!"

"They do have lovely fleece," Robert added as he brought the horses back down to feed them in their stalls. "The Scots-Irish will love that for weaving. There are a lot of weavers here in the valley, and they'll be delighted with the wool from these sheep."

"They're fierce-looking animals, even without horns," Old Cyrus observed. "They're also half-wild because they've been turned out in the mountains away from people. They could make a formidable opponent for a dog Monty's size, or even Danny's. Yet the dogs look determined to herd the rams the same way they've herded the ewes."

The men watched with interest as Monty backed the half-wild rams step-by-step down to the stream. They never turned their backs on the determined dog. When they finally reached the stream, they stopped to drink their fill of the cold mountain water.

"Sheep can be stupid animals," Cyrus said, as he took out his pipe. He studied it carefully, then knocked it against the gate and returned it to his pocket. Danny appeared uninterested in sheep as he lay beside Cyrus.

"Yes, but these sheep could upgrade my flock and provide mutton and fleece. I hope they've been a good investment," Robert commented.

"They are a good 'estment if you axed me," Old Cyrus said, offering his opinion. "I still think those rams will be more than Monty or even Danny can handle. They won't be herded as easily as the ewes running wild in the mountains."

Monty tried to bring the rams downstream closer to the cabin, where Spotted Deer stood watching them with interest. He'd cleaned out the cabin and was sweeping the front porch, but he paused to watch the rams and Monty circle each other.

"What shall I call them?" Robert asked Cyrus, as they swept up the scattered pieces of hay and finished their chores with the horses.

"Those rams are going to be trouble. Monty can barely herd them. I ain't all that excited about their arrival for all the work they'll give us. What names will express their kind of trouble?"

"What about Oliver Cromwell?" Robert suggested. From Welsh history, he knew of Cromwell's repressive Puritan government in the $17^{th}$ century.

"No, we need something more American," Charlie replied. "Something from our own history."

"I shall call these rams Banastre Tarleton and Lord General Cornwallis. Those fellers gave us real trouble not so long ago at the Battle of Cowpens," Old Cyrus proclaimed. "That's a fine set of names for these rams. We can call that fierce-looking one Benny for short—the same nickname Daniel Morgan gave to Colonel Tarleton."

## OCTOBER

When the frost covered the mountains, Robert got up early to attend to his stock. The fire coals from the previous night still burned low upon the hearth. He hummed a Welsh tune he'd learned in his childhood as he stepped gingerly around Old Cyrus and Danny, both asleep in front of the new chimney after a hard day's work finishing it.

Robert put a log on the dying fire before he let himself out into the cold morning. Old Cyrus snored softly, and Spotted Deer hardly moved in the loft above him. These were the mornings that Robert liked best—frosty and solitary.

The birds chattered in the trees as they made plans to fly south for the winter. The ground felt hard beneath Robert's feet when he washed from a bucket of icy water. He shivered as he dried his face and hands.

A buzzard flew overhead, looking for carrion. An owl hooted from his tree before he settled down for his daily nap. Robert looked up and saw an old hawk's nest. A hawk circled above him as he walked up to the barn by the path beside the stream. He fed the horses and let the troublesome sheep out before he fed the chickens.

"*Cock-a-doodle doo*," sang the young rooster. "*How are you?*"

Robert laughed. "Good morning, Glendower, and how are you?" He loved these early mornings on the farm. There was something magical about the frost and the rime on the trees.

"I wish Sarah could see it," Robert mused. "If only she could get used to living in America. Annie and Ellen have settled in well so far. What will we do if Sarah never settles?"

He rarely expressed these secret fears, but his concern for Sarah's happiness nagged at his conscience.

Her inability to cope with a new language and a new country cast a shadow over his otherwise optimistic morning.

Daniel Morgan nickered as Robert opened the stall door to give him his ration of oats. Light Horse Harry pushed against his door, impatient to be fed.

"There you go, now, Harry. Here's your breakfast." He patted the horse's thickening winter coat. "You'll have to learn some good manners."

Danny, upon awakening, pushed open the cabin's front door and ran toward Robert for his breakfast. Robert fed the dog and let out the ewes. The dog guided them to the pasture and came back to tackle the two rams, Tarleton and Cornwallis. Still unused to being handled, they rushed past the dog and headed for the stream.

As dawn broke, Robert fed his chickens and gathered their eggs. "It must be near breakfast time 'cause I feel hungry," he said aloud. The sun was up and cast shadows across the frosty landscape. Although Robert shivered, he felt invigorated and happy to be on his farm. He hoped that Sarah would also find comfort there.

It was a busy autumn, with so many new animals in his care. The list now included sheep, two cows, two horses, and a dog. Old Cyrus and Spotted Deer had slowly made the barn and the cabin more homelike and secure. They also had staked out a garden plot for the spring.

The trees put on their autumn finery. The oaks, maples, elms, and walnuts were red and yellow. The pines and cedars appeared regal in their dark green, and the mountains became rich with color. The nights grew cold and dark. A thick mirror-like coating of ice appeared on the rain barrels in the mornings.

Robert met Charlie and Yorweth at the stock sales, and Yorweth's farm, although not as pretty a piece of land as Robert's, looked more settled. His house slowly progressed from a two-room dwelling into a small traditional Shenandoah Valley I-house.

October's brisk days settled into November's chill. Charlie came up and the men helped Robert chop firewood for the winter. The last of the wild geese flew south in their distinctive V formation, and the small animals hibernated. The foxes and the dogs barked at night as the days of the late autumn ended and winter began, promising snow.

## OLD CYRUS'S TALES OF WAR

"I wish you'd tell us a story, Mr. Cyrus," Zack coaxed. "It's a good storytelling time. I likes to hear your tales of the War of Independence and General Cornwallis."

"Don't forget to tell us where you fought the British," Tommy added. "Don't forget the 'Swampy Fox' and the marshes of the Santee."

Pleased that the boys wanted to hear his stories, Cyrus took a swig of moonshine, cleared his throat, and began with the Battle of Cowpens.

"It was January 17, 1781, after the Battle of King's Mountain, where the Americans routed the British and killed Major Ferguson. We who lived in the mountains of what became Buncombe County, North Carolina, wanted to join the Patriots' Militia.

"Sam, our neighbor, got us fired up about hit. He also showed showed my brother, Joseph, and me how to march and to follow commands. He drilled us up and back across my father's farmyard, and we shot off our Kentucky long rifles just like real soldiers. We scared the hens out of a week's egg laying."

"You've got it," John assured us as we presented arms and did a short-order drill and parade dressed like a professional soldier.

"What will General Morgan say if he finds out we are only sixteen and Joseph's eighteen?'

"They don't care," Sam told us. "They have boys in the army younger than you. Other fellas will be going down to join, so the officers won't care how old you are as long as you can shoot straight."

"We've heard of "Benny" Tarleton and his cruel ways of killin' prisoners and of raidin' the farms of the Patriots and stealin' their horses, cattle, and other supplies. He's a professional soldier, and we don't want no truck with him."

Old Cyrus finished the lunch Carrie provided him. He opened his jug, but seeing that it was empty, he put it down.

"Would you like some more cider?" Robert offered as they sat before the dying fire.

"My mama made it from fresh apples from the farmers' market," Tommy said. "It's good and will wet your throat for storytelling."

Cyrus took a swig of the cider and cleared his throat. It didn't have much kick, but it was wet and cooled his voice box so he could put on his storyteller's voice and begin.

"All three of us decided to go down the mountain and join the Patriots' Militia under Colonel Andrew Pickens. We left Buncombe County early one morning before sunup without informin' Pa and rode three ponies, too light for farm work, to go and fight with General Daniel Morgan.

"He was an old Indian fighter with General Washington during the French and Indian war with Canada. Daniel Morgan was a famous rugged old soldier who bore a most marvelest scar from a bullet wound in his jaw. That bullet entered his jaw and knocked all his teeth out on one side. It was a wonderful scar and showed Daniel Morgan to be a veteran warrior.

"We crossed the French Broad River into South Carolina. There's a place called Hannah's Cowpens about three miles on the other side of the state line. It was here that cattle were given salt and were rounded up and marked for ownership. Hit was the place that the Battle of Cowpens was fought.

"The ground was hilly and because of the cattle's grazin' there was little undergrowth, but an open woody place. The ground dipped gently before hit rose on the other side.

"General Morgan and Lieutenant Colonel John Howard led the Maryland and Delaware Continentals with rifleman under Major Triplett and the light dragoons, or mounted infantry, under Lieutenant Colonel William Washington. These were regular troops and not tag-alongs as were the over-mountain-boys like Joseph, Sam, and me.

"General Nathanael Greene came south to take over General Gates's job. He had almost lost the Carolinas, but General Greene knew his business and soon had things hopping with men like the 'Old Wagoneer,' Daniel Morgan, and that sly fox of the swamps, Francis Marion."

Old Cyrus paused to drink his cider and to catch his breath.

"This isn't as tasty as my corn whiskey, but it's good to wet my parched throat," he half complained, grateful for a cup of something wet. Then he continued with his story.

"General Greene split his force and sent one group eastward toward the Pee Dee River and Charlestown. Here he would link up with Francis Marion and 'Gamecock Sumter,' who had been wounded and was recovering in the western part of South Carolina.

"It was a pretty brave thing to do. Most generals wouldn't have split their forces. But then, Daniel Morgan and General Greene ain't most generals.

"This action made Lord Cornwallis split his forces to cover both ends of South Carolina.

"Betwixt the four little armies we had some right smart battles. Nobody is more careful about battlefields than Daniel Morgan. He studies the lay of the ground, the hills, and valleys. He knows the cover, the woody places with trees and rocks where we could hide. He knows where the rivers were to hold up your leaving. He knows the ground if it's marshy or dry. He studied them things. The field at Cowpens suited Morgan. He was a tactician and knowed his men's ability to get off two shots and retire into the woods. Then the next company of militia did the same.

"Benny Tarleton just drove his troops into an assault and hacked with their swords. General Greene and Daniel Morgan placed their men to the best advantage. Morgan believed it was best to surprise folks like Benny Tarleton and get them disorganized. That's exactly what General Morgan did at Cowpens. We won in less than an hour because we had organization and smart generals."

"Most of the men from the mountains knowed little about fightin' in an army way. But we could shoot and knowed how to take cover and reload in a hurry. Colonel Pickens told us to tie our ponies up and to fight on foot. He would tell us what to do. He did, and we followed his commands just like in Pa's farm yard drill."

## THE RACE TO THE DAN

A few days later Carrie sent Zack and Tommy out to visit Robert and to take him a home-cooked dinner. After the boys arrived and helped Robert on the farm, they savored the wonderful homemade bread and stew that Carrie had made and settled down for an hour of storytelling.

"Mr. Cyrus," Tommy asked the old man. "Tell us some more stories about your war adventures and about Francis Marion, the Swamp Fox."

"Do tell us a story about General Daniel Morgan and General Nathanael Greene and how they fought the British." Zack added to their wish list of tales. So Old Cyrus made himself comfortable and after pouring himself some moonshine whiskey and wetting his parched throat, he pretended to have forgotten all of his adventures. Then suddenly, he remembered and began.

"Oh, they were interesting times. Let's see.... Where should I begin?

"In his race to the Dan River and the Virginia border, Daniel Morgan didn't linger after the Battle of Cowpens in South Carolina.

"He got us up to march north before dawn of January 18. We had 600 British prisoners and all our own gear to move out. We had broke the back of Colonel Tarleton's expeditionary force in less than an hour. Now we headed north to link up with General Greene and to cross the Dan River and resupply our army on the boundary with Virginia.

"General Greene had maps made of the many creeks and rivers which crisscrossed North and South Carolina. He understood the toppography of the pine barrens and the rivers with their many forks and streams.

"Later that day, Cornwallis got some reinforcements from Charlestown and set out after Morgan's 'flying army.' We were by that time twenty miles away from Cowpens.

"I don't think General Cornwallis ever understood the many rivers and creeks or the red clay which clings like glue on equipment and tears shoes to pieces and makes horses slide and fall. I've seen three stout horses fall into the mud because their wagon wheels were up to the axles in red clay.

"Lord Cornwallis never understood the stickiness of red clay or the strength of that clay. He never understood about the rivers and the wet, marshy land. General Greene knowed how to move equipment through it without gettin' it stuck or lost.

"He understood the pine barrens and their spooky trees with black trunks and their dark green needles which covered the land.

"One British prisoner told me that he knowed ghosts walked among them dark trees.

"'I'm sure they do,'" he insisted. 'Especially on moonless nights when there are no stars, and the owls are hooting and the foxes are barking. It's enough to frighten the best of us.'

"I don't think Lord Cornwallis understood country life.

"He was too anxious to burn houses and to steal horses and cattle. He'd string up the owner of the farm and leave the family to perish in the flames. The loyalists turned against him, and Cornwallis and 'Benny' Tarleton found few friends in the Carolinas."

Old Cyrus continued with his story.

"At the River Dan we said good-bye to General Morgan. That was sad, but his piles were so bad he could not sit a horse; his arthritis was so painful he could find no more ease from it. General Greene found a coach and a grand pair of stout horses and a detail of several men to carry him back to the Shenandoah Valley.

"Nathanael Greene had tears in his eyes as he wished the old warrior good-bye: 'Great Generals are rare. There are few Morgans to be found.'

"His friend, Otho Williams took over the command and after waving the old warrior off and wishing him God's speed we marched to Jennings Ordinary to find fresh horses and equipment. We found shoes. Ours were worn out from marching from Cowpens in the rain and red clay at one mile an hour on little food. General von Steuben had trained militia who replaced our tired, half-starved troops from Cowpens. My feet were warm and dry at last. I had food in my belly, so I could not complain. I also had a dry uniform. I felt lucky, and thanked Virginia's plentiful land for providing it."

"General Greene decided to meet Cornwallis at Guilford Courthouse. Guilford was a Quaker settlement, and the land was suitable for a battlefield. Greene's troops were outnumbered, but with Light Horse Harry Lee's cavalry and William Washington's mounted infantry Greene decided to meet the British. That battle cost the British dear, and Cornwallis moved east to Wilmington on the coast. Then he went to Virginia and got bottled up on Gloucester Point and retreated to Yorktown Island, where he mistook the French fleet for the British one and lost the war. He and Benny Tarleton finally went back to England and left us in peace."

Cyrus took another swig of his cider and shifted his position because his leg had gone to sleep.

"That's a pretty good story," said Zack, smiling. "Now, finish it—and be sure it's all true."

"Let me tell you how I met Francis Marion, the Swamp Fox. After the Battle of Guilford, we went into South Carolina. In the confusion, I became lost from my militia group. I didn't know which way to go when a slave man nearly ran over me riding a sorrel horse and leading two others.

"'What you doin' thar?' he yelled at me, and I jumped into the ditch.

"'Lookin' for my friends,' I replied as I caught myself from falling. You near 'bout run me down.'

"'Can't you ride a horse?' the man demanded. "If you want to see some real fightin', come with me.'

"'Where to?' I asked.

"'You ever heard of Francis Marion? The one the British call The Swamp Fox?'

"The man pulled his horses to a halt. 'Git on that bay hoss, and I'll take you to him. You'll sure enough do some fightin'. Can you ride a hoss?'

"'I was raised on a farm,' I replied. 'I can ride most anything.'

"I caught the bay horse and the slave handed me the reins. I jumped onto the muddy saddle, and we rode through the swamp jus' aflyin'. There was nary a sound under that horse's feet.

"We rode for several miles through the swamps of the Santee River and swam across the water to Snow Island, Marion's headquarters.

"I never saw such a group of men. They wore caps with white plumes, and their clothes looked clean. No fleas or lice on these men.

"'I brought you a lost soul,' the Negro man told the wiry little General who limped from bad ankles and knees. 'An' I brought two good horses I captured from the British.'

"I guessed I was the lost soul. I certainly was lost in all that swampy place."

"'Can you shoot a gun?' Marion demanded. 'What you got to shoot?'

"'A Kentucky rifle,' I replied. 'I growed up in the North Carolina mountains, and I can shoot straight.'

"'You see those men over there?' Marion pointed to the leader of a small band of men. 'You join them. That's Peter Horry. Now go wash and get some shoes on your feet.'

"Peter Horry took me to wash and found some boots to fit my frozen feet."

"'You come along with us. Where you from?' he demanded.

"'The North Carolina Mountains,' I said. 'I got separated from my militia group after Guilford Courthouse because my feet was froze. And since I had no footwear, I met Joe, and he give me a horse to ride, and I come along with him.'

"Peter Horry kept me in South Carolina for a couple of weeks. Then he told me I needed to get back to my own outfit or I could be shot as a deserter. He fixed it up, and I rejoined my own group after the most exciting time of my life. General Marion kept things happening right smart, and although he had gammy knees and ankles, nobody could outride Marion through the Santee Swamps and Pee Dee River. He kept the British hopping and pushed them out of South Carolina to Charlestown. There, the British navy picked them up. Fightin' with him and Peter Horry was extra special."

The three men leaned over the gate and watched as Monty and the sheep challenged each other. The rams faced the dog and stood firm as Monty tried to herd them farther downstream.

"Yes," said Cyrus, humming an old tune. Then he sang it somewhat off-key and shuffled his feet in a dance step he'd learned as a boy in the North Carolina mountains:

> *Cornwallis led a country dance,*
> *The like was never seen, sir;*
> *Much retrograde and much advance,*
> *And all with General Greene, sir.*
> *They rambled up and rambled down,*
> *Joined hands and off they ran, sir;*
> *General Greene marched to old Charlestown*
> *As Cornwallis fled to Wilmington, sir.*

"It doesn't scan very well," Charlie remarked. "Did you make it up, Cyrus?"

"No, somebody else did at the time. Only he left out Tarleton. I guess it doesn't rhyme with much else."

Old Cyrus continued to shuffle his feet in a dance, and nearly upset Charlie when Cyrus swung him around in a do-si-do before they went back to the gate to retrieve his pipe.

"Here you are." Robert picked up the lost pipe and handed it to Cyrus, laughing. "You act like Daniel Morgan and Light Horse Harry Lee all rolled into one, My Lord of the Valley."

## ANDREW JACKSON'S ELECTION

"What's going on with those squirrels in Washington?" Old Cyrus demanded. "They run around and around and do nothing. They are meaner and crazier than ever!"

Charlie shrugged. "I can't see Old Hickory in office with his backwoods crowd running our country. Andrew Jackson was a good soldier, but I don't fancy him as our president."

"The Battle of New Orleans was a great victory with that French pirate, Jean Lafitte, and his savage crews manning eight ships and blocking the Gulf of Mexico and the entrance into the Mississippi River," Spotted Deer said. "But who wants a bunch of unruly pirates running our country?"

They sat around the kitchen fire and tried to solve the nation's election problems. Charlie had stopped by Mrs. Taylor's to pick up the two boys to bring them out to see Mr. Robert's farm.

"Jackson's defensive position at the Battle of New Orleans included frontiersmen from the hills of Tennessee and eastern Kentucky. A wilder bunch of fighters you'd never seen," Old Cyrus explained as he gave the boys some hot chocolate and offered Charlie and Robert some more coffee. "Jackson's troops included some dandified Creoles, some freed slaves, and some fierce Choctaw Indians."

"And the French pirate Lafitte and his crews, who had been pardoned if they promised to fight for the Americans," Tommy explained. "I read about the pirates in a book Mrs. Glynis loaned me."

"Yes," agreed Charlie. "But the British troops came to the battle in a field full of sugar cane stubble, which offered them no protection from artillery fire. They lost over 2,000 men. The American losses were small. The British wear red coats and don't fight Indian-style behind trees and in the woods. Americans don't fight in an open field."

"Who thought that up?" Zack inquired. "To fight with no cover."

"It all goes back to the early British style of fighting," Charlie explained as he got up to leave. "I still don't want Andrew Jackson as president and his motley crew running the government in Washington."

"That's like a bug arguing with a chicken," quipped Cyrus.

## TROUBLE AT THE BOARDING HOUSE

Although Charlie's visit in September had cheered her briefly, Sarah's homesickness soon returned. Robert's requests for Sarah to visit the farm were constantly met with tears and protests. By December, Sarah had still refused to see the cabin, and Annie and Ellen were exhausted and worried. Not sure what else to do, they asked Carrie to call for Mrs. Glynis, in the hope that she might be able to convince their mother to change her mind.

"Zack," Carrie called to her son. "Go and find Mrs. Glynis and ask her to come over here. Miss Annie and Miss Ellen need her."

Zack ran off like a shot, with Tommy following behind him. Mrs. Glynis and her sister and their friends lived over on Boscowan Street, not far from the boarding house.

Zack walked up to the back door of Mrs. Glynis' house and knocked.

"What is it, Zack?" Mrs. Glynis asked when she opened the door and saw the two boys.

"My mama told me to tell you that Miss Annie and Miss Ellen need you. Mrs. Jones is still refusing to go visit the new farm that Mr. Robert worked so hard on, and Miss Annie is in tears," the boy said in almost one breath.

"Can I play the piano for Miss Gwynn?" Tommy asked, excited by the prospect.

"Come in, and I'll call her," Mrs. Glynis offered as Tommy entered her house.

Miss Gwynn came downstairs. Then she and Tommy retired to the sitting room for a piano lesson while Mrs. Glynis and Zack walked back to the boarding house. On their way, Zack explained the situation.

"Mrs. Jones is determined to go back to Wales," he told Mrs. Glynis. "But it's across the sea and everything is sold, and Mr. Robert can't work in the mines anymore. She has to stay here."

"I know," said Mrs. Glynis. "It's sad."

"Mr. Cyrus told us that the farm is really beautiful now, and he worked so hard to help Spotted Deer and Mr. Robert finish the cabin before autumn came and the nights got cold."

Zack let himself into the kitchen and held the door for Mrs. Glynis. In the parlor, they found Annie, sipping her second cup of tea.

Carrie came in after them and offered Mrs. Glynis a cup of tea from Granny's teapot.

"Yes, please, Carrie," she replied. "That would be nice."

"Thank you for coming," Annie said. "I don't know what we shall do. Mother still refuses to go out to see the farm."

"I know, dear. Your mother is very homesick," Mrs. Glynis said as she sat down beside Annie and drank her tea.

"I hoped Mother would want to please my father and would try to help him. Now that he can't work in the mines, farming on good land seemed an opportunity for them both. We've sold everything in Wales. We can't go back. Oh, why can't Mother settle and be happy?" Annie burst into tears.

"Is the cabin ready?" Mrs. Glynis asked. She put her cup on a table and took Annie's hand.

"Yes."

"Why don't one of you girls go to the country with your father? Then Sarah could stay here with the other one and visit the farm now and then. That way, she could get used to it gradually."

"I had hoped to move out to the farm, but if Mother isn't going to move out there . . ." Annie stopped, unable to finish.

"Where is Mr. Jones now?" Mrs. Glynis asked.

"He and Yorweth went to the tavern," Annie

replied. "Papa is crushed at Mother's response. You could see it in his face. He's worked so hard."

"Maybe tomorrow will be better. Maybe your mother is just tired. Tomorrow we will come over for tea and see if we can help convince her that it will be all right. How does that sound?" Mrs. Glynis offered. "Now, dry your tears. I'll come over tomorrow."

"That would be fine. I'll let Carrie know," Annie said, with a faint smile. "What else can we do? Maybe it will work."

The next day, the four Welsh women—Mrs. Glynis, Miss Gwynn, Efa, and Anwen—came for tea. As they sat in the parlor talking, Sarah appeared tired and listless. She drank a cup of tea, but refused any cakes. "I want to remain in town and not go live in the country," she announced. "It's lonely in the country. I'm not going," she stated firmly. "I do not feel well. I am going to my room." She got up and left the parlor. The four Welsh women sat in silence, wondering what to do.

"I'll go check on her," Annie offered, and headed up the stairs behind her mother.

With their visit cut short, Mrs. Glynis and her companions excused themselves and went home. Ellen then followed Annie upstairs. After several minutes, however, they both came running back down.

"Carrie, Carrie!" cried Ellen. "Where is Mrs. Taylor? Mother is burning up with fever. She appears terribly sick."

"Mrs. Taylor has gone to the market," Carrie replied. "I'll send Zack for Dr. Mason. His office is not far."

Ellen burst into tears, terrified at the thought of losing her mother.

"You go back to her, Miss Ellen, and I'll get some cold water from the springhouse to make compresses for her head. Zack, run like the wind to Dr. Mason's and get him to come. Miss Sarah is ill. Quickly now, don't stop for anything," said Carrie. Zack left the porch as fast as he could.

Carrie then turned to Tommy. "Tommy, go to the springhouse at the end of the garden and get me some cold water." She handed the boy a big metal pitcher.

By the time Tommy returned with the water, Carrie and Annie had already cut up some old towels to make compresses. Carrie took the pitcher, and Annie carried the towels. They ran upstairs. Carrie knocked gently on Sarah's bedroom door and found her lying on the bed, tossing and turning. Her dress and sheets were wet with perspiration. Quickly, Carrie applied compresses to Sarah's forehead with the wet, cold towels. Annie helped Carrie remove Sarah's dress and put her in a clean nightgown.

Ellen sat in tears beside her mother's bed. Carrie shook her head.

"Miss Ellen, dry your eyes and help me with these compresses. You can rinse them in the water for me. They need to be cold, so we have to change them every few minutes. Does Miss Sarah feel any cooler to you?"

"Oh, Carrie," cried the usually reserved Ellen. "I'm afraid. I'm very much afraid."

"Shh, shh," warned Annie, keeping a more level head. "She can hear you. Do as Carrie tells you. I'll go downstairs, now. I think I hear Zack with the doctor."

Annie left the room and ran down the stairs. Zack and Dr. Mason were just coming in the front door as she reached the parlor.

"Oh, Dr. Mason," Annie gasped. "I'm so glad you came. My mother is burning up with fever. Please come on upstairs. Zack, we'll need more cool water. Can you bring us another containerful?"

"Yes, ma'am," Zack replied as he went to the kitchen for another large pitcher. "Tommy, come and help me fetch some spring water," he called to his brother.

Annie led Dr. Mason upstairs to the sickroom. Ellen still sat by the bed crying while Carrie put compresses on Sarah's head, trying to cool her body temperature.

Ellen got up as Dr. Mason entered. "Thank goodness you're here," she whispered. "Mama is awfully sick."

He looked grim as he examined Sarah. "You've done the right thing to try to get her fever down," he told Carrie. "You're a good nurse. I remember when Mrs. Taylor was ill, and you nursed her."

"Thank you, sir." Carrie picked up her wet towels with the pitcher of water and prepared to leave.

"We'll need more spring water," said Dr. Mason.

"It's coming," said Annie.

"Good," replied the doctor as he walked with Ellen to the door. "Now, dry your eyes," he told her. "You can be a lot more help to your mother if you stop crying. She is gravely ill. I believe it's pneumonia, and it's serious. Annie, keep the cold compresses changed. When Carrie returns, tell her to wash your mother's arms and legs, too. That's another way to reduce fever. Where's your father?"

"Out on the farm. He's been there since yesterday trying to get the cabin finished for Mama to move into. Old Cyrus and Spotted Deer are with him," Ellen said as she dried her tears.

"Hmmm. Can you ride a horse?" Dr. Mason suddenly asked her

"Not well, but Annie can. Why?" Ellen replied.

"Tell Annie to come up here at once. I need to speak with her," Dr. Mason commanded.

Ellen dashed down the stairs. "Annie, Dr. Mason wants you," she called to her sister.

"I'm coming. Carrie's finding me some clean towels, and she'll come up, too."

"I'll bring the water," Ellen told her sister.

Annie fled up the stairs and arrived in the sickroom

out of breath.

"Can you ride a horse?" Dr. Mason wanted to know.

"Yes, I can," Annie replied. "Charlie taught me on the wagon train, and I used to ride Adams around the pasture in the evenings."

"Good. I have two saddle horses and a groom to accompany you to the farm. You must go and tell your father that your mother is gravely ill and to come at once."

"Is she that bad?" Annie whispered. "Is she going to die?"

"I hope not," replied Dr. Mason. "But your father needs to be here. And Ellen seems to have a natural affinity for nursing. Can you ride a horse well enough to go and get him?"

"I can," Annie said firmly.

"Then Golden Eagle, my stable groom, will accompany you to the farm. He's part Indian and has an Indian name. Does your father have a horse to ride back on?"

"Yes, Old Cyrus loaned him Light Horse Harry."

"Good. Now get changed, and go at once. Do you know anyone who can come here to help Carrie and Ellen?"

"Yes," said Annie. "Mrs. Glynis. She speaks Welsh. Mother prefers it to English."

"You get changed, I'll send Zack to bring Mrs. Glynis," Dr. Mason told Annie. "Tommy can go to my house to tell Golden Eagle to saddle the horses and bring them here. Where's Carrie?"

"Here I am, Dr. Mason," said Carrie as she entered the sick room, bringing a heavy pitcher of spring water. Ellen followed her, carrying more clean towels.

"I'm sending Annie out to fetch your father," Dr. Mason told Ellen. "Golden Eagle, my groom, will bring two horses ready to go. Does your sister ride sidesaddle?"

"No," replied a surprised Ellen. "She's never had any saddle. She just rode bareback." Ellen was puzzled by the question.

"She'll have to ride sidesaddle through town, and once in the country she can do as she likes. She must go for your father right away." Dr. Mason knocked on Annie's door. "Are you ready?"

"I guess so." Annie appeared, dressed in cast-off riding clothes she had collected from various places after they came to Winchester.

"That will do, I suppose." Dr. Mason looked at her, surprised at the semi-respectable riding habit Annie had found. "Now, Golden Eagle should be here any minute."

Annie and Dr. Mason went downstairs and out into the front garden. Zack and Golden Eagle arrived a few minutes later with the horses. Golden Eagle rode a big black hunter, Marcus, and Zack sat awkwardly on the sidesaddle on Paint, an agile pony.

"This is Miss Annie, Golden Eagle," Dr. Mason said. "She'll guide you to her father's farm a few miles west of here. He has a horse there he can ride. Tell him his wife is gravely ill and is in danger. Ask a neighbor to feed his stock—he needs to come to town as soon as possible. Now, Annie, you must go."

He helped her into the saddle and showed her how to place her right leg over the pommel. Then he sent her and Golden Eagle on their way. He knew that as soon as Annie left Winchester's prying eyes, she would probably ride astride and they would make better time.

Annie felt very uncomfortable riding sidesaddle, but she endured it until they left the town behind. Then she threw her right leg over Paint and rode him astride as she had done when she rode Adams in the pasture in the evenings.

Golden Eagle was very clever with horses. He led them out of Winchester toward the mountains.

Meanwhile, Dr. Mason went back to his patient. A few minutes later, Zack opened the front door for Mrs. Glynis and Tommy.

"I understand that Mrs. Jones is very ill," she said. "I've come to help."

"Yes, ma'am," Zack replied, as he held the door ajar for her. "The doctor is with Miss Sarah now. She's got a bad fever. They sent for Mr. Robert, so she must be very ill."

Mrs. Glynis went upstairs and found Dr. Mason, Carrie, and Ellen gathered around Sarah's bedside. Ellen's eyes were red from crying, and Dr. Mason appeared grave.

He looked up and saw the visitor in the doorway. "Ah, Mrs. Glynis, come in. We're trying to get Mrs. Jones's temperature down."

"What can I do to help?" Mrs. Glynis asked.

"Take Ellen downstairs for a cup of tea. She's worn out and needs a rest. Carrie and I can manage well enough for now. Ask Zack or Tommy to bring up more spring water."

"Come, Ellen." Mrs. Glynis took her downstairs. Once out of her mother's room, Ellen's tears started afresh and blinded her, causing her to trip. Mrs. Glynis caught her and led her into the warm kitchen to have some tea.

Meanwhile, Annie rode astride on the pony, anxious to reach her father. Golden Eagle pushed Marcus to walk faster as Annie trotted on Paint to keep up with them. Even though the road was rough and stony, they made good progress. Finally, after about an hour they reached the farm.

"Cyrus," Annie called from the ridge above the barn. "Old Cyrus, can you hear me?" Danny, Cyrus's faithful dog, barked and ran up the path toward the visitors.

Spotted Deer saw the two horses and waved, not recognizing their riders.

"Spotted Deer," Annie called. "Where's my father?"

"Down by the creek," the Indian lad replied. "He's gone fishing."

Annie spurred the pony forward and trotted down the ridge to the barn. "Mother's very ill and Dr. Mason sent me to fetch Papa. Where is the borrowed horse?"

Old Cyrus ran to the pasture and caught Light Horse Harry while Spotted Deer hurried down to the creek to find Robert.

Robert looked up from his fishing and drew in his line as Spotted Deer reached him, then waited expectantly.

"Your daughter Annie is here," the Indian lad called as he ran through the woods. "She's come to take you back to Winchester. Your wife, Miss Sarah, is ill. Dr. Mason wants you to come right away," Spotted Deer said breathlessly. "It will be dark in an hour. Old Cyrus is saddling Light Horse Harry for you to ride."

Robert followed the Indian back to the barn, where Old Cyrus had saddled Harry and put on his bridle.

"What's wrong with your mother?" Robert asked Annie when she galloped Paint up the path beside the creek to meet him.

"She has a high fever, and she's gravely ill. Dr. Mason sent me to fetch you." Annie and Robert returned to the barn, as Danny followed behind, barking for them to hurry.

Old Cyrus held Harry and gave Robert a boost to reach the saddle. "It must be serious if Miss Annie and Golden Eagle have both come to fetch you," Old Cyrus warned Robert.

Robert gathered up Harry's reins, and Cyrus led him up the path and onto the road. Spotted Deer waved them good-bye, and the three travelers were soon out of sight.

"It sounds very grave," Old Cyrus said to Spotted Deer after they had gone. He returned to his stool, and Danny again lay at his feet.

"It will be dark before they get back to Winchester," Spotted Deer replied. "Yes, Miss Sarah must be bad off to send both Annie and Golden Eagle."

"It feels like snow tonight," he said, looking at the sky.

Meanwhile, Annie and Robert rode at a trot behind Marcus, Golden Eagle's big hunter. They hurried to reach Winchester before it became too dark to see the road. Golden Eagle hung a lantern on his saddle, and he carried a set of bells for each of the horses. Robert also carried a lantern as he and Harry followed Annie on Paint.

"Evenings come early by December," Golden Eagle observed as he hurried on at a good pace, anxious to return before night overtook them. After that, no one spoke as they rode single file across the mountains in the darkening landscape. When the sun set, the evening became bitterly cold, and a gentle snow began to fall.

In Winchester, Dr. Mason, Ellen, and Carrie worked to bring Sarah's fever down. When he thought she was cooler, Dr. Mason prepared to leave.

"Send for me again if you need me," he told Mrs. Glynis. "I'm going home for now. I'll call in the morning to see how things are progressing."

"Yes, go on home, Doctor," Mrs. Glynis assured him. "I can manage with Carrie and Ellen. I'll send Zack or Tommy if we need you."

"Annie should be back soon. It's twilight now, and I see the lamplighter on the street. So Winchester won't be entirely dark."

"If Miss Sarah needs your care, I'll send one of the boys. Go on home now. You must be tired," Mrs. Glynis encouraged him.'

"I'll be back in the morning," Dr. Mason promised.

"I'll walk down with you, Doctor." Mrs. Glynis left the bedside to accompany the tired man down the stairs to the front door.

"Annie should be back soon," the doctor promised. "The farm isn't too far away."

"Yes," said Mrs. Glynis. "They'll come directly. Sarah doesn't feel as hot as she did earlier, so I hope she's getting better. I'd be glad for Mr. Jones to see her now."

The doctor let himself out. Mrs. Glynis stood in the doorway and watched him go down the street as the lamplighter lit his lamp at the corner.

"Zack, Tommy, come here," Mrs. Glynis called to the boys.

The two children entered the hall from the kitchen. "Yes, ma'am," they replied. "Here we are."

Zack looked worried. "Is Miss Sarah any better?"

"She appears to be," Mrs. Glynis replied. "When Miss Annie returns, you and Tommy will go with Golden Eagle to take the pony home."

"Yes, ma'am," said Zack. "We'll be here to help you."

"Thank you. I knew I could count on you," Mrs. Glynis replied, before she turned to go back upstairs. "You boys get something to eat now."

"Yes, ma'am, we will. Mama left dinner for us. Come on, Tommy." Zack and his younger brother entered their mother's kitchen to find their dinner.

## SNOW

It was dark when Annie and Robert arrived. Golden Eagle brought them to Mrs. Taylor's house and told Zack he could lead both the pony and Light Horse Harry himself.

"I can manage," Golden Eagle insisted. "Zack needs to stay here in case the doctor is wanted."

"I am tired," said Annie, as she jumped down from the pony. "Come, Papa, let's go see how Mother is feeling."

Mrs. Glynis appeared at the door and welcomed the travelers. "Come in," she said. "We are glad you're here. Mrs. Taylor says she has prepared dinner for you."

"Oh, thank you," said Annie, greatly relieved. "I am starving after that long trip. Thank you so much, Mrs. Taylor. You are wonderful."

"Your mother's a little better, so come in and relax before you go up to see her. Come in and eat something," Mrs. Taylor welcomed them.

Robert paid her no attention as he ran up the stairs to his wife's room. "How is she, Carrie?" he asked.

"She's better than she was," Carrie replied. "We's glad you is here."

At first, Robert didn't see Ellen slumped in a chair, sound asleep. She was partly hidden by the open door. Robert spoke to his wife in Welsh; she opened her eyes and gave a wan smile.

"Looks like Miss Sarah is better," Carrie whispered. "She's been waiting for you."

"I'll go down to dinner now," Robert said. "Then I'll come back to talk to Sarah."

After a good meal with Annie, Robert took the pitcher of warm water Zack offered him and went upstairs to wash before he entered Sarah's room again. Mrs. Glynis sent Carrie down for supper and remained with the sick woman. Robert returned and sat in the chair by Sarah's bed.

"You go on down," he offered. "I'm with her now."

"No," Mrs. Glynis insisted. "I'll stay with you for a while."

They sat in silence for several minutes. Ellen remained asleep in the cozy chair, and Annie looked in quickly, then went to change her clothes.

"I'll come back," she promised, but long hours in the uncomfortable sidesaddle had exhausted her. Soon she fell asleep on her bed, her unusual riding habit discarded and the boots she'd worn placed neatly beside a chair.

Robert and Mrs. Glynis sat watching Sarah for a long time without speaking. Sarah dozed fitfully, and her temperature rose once again, in spite of the cold compresses.

The December evening was dark. It was still snowing outside. Mrs. Glynis got up to put another log on the grate when the flame almost went out. She built up the fire with a little coal, and soon the room felt warmer.

Robert whispered to Sarah in Welsh as he sat beside her bed holding her hand. "Do you remember the valleys, Sarah, when the men sang in chorus? Such grand voices they had. We made the town ring with song."

"Ah," he sighed. "We had great companions in those days, many loyal friends and neighbors. There were hard times, too, but what wonderful music we all shared in the valleys."

Sarah opened her eyes. "Yes," she said. "I remember."

Robert hummed a Welsh tune he knew Sarah liked and then sang the words, stumbling over them as if long forgotten.

*Arlan y môr mae rhosys cochion*
(Beside the sea there are red roses)
*Arlan y môr mae lilis gwynnion*
(Beside the sea there are lovely lilies)

*Arlan y môr mae 'nghariad inne*
(Beside the sea my sweetheart lives)
*Yn cysgu'r nos a chodi'r bore.*
(Asleep at night and awake at morning.)

Sarah smiled at Robert. "*Ar Lan y Môr*," she said, recalling the title immediately. "I remember," she whispered. "How well I remember." She closed her eyes. "Aye, those were happy times."

It continued snowing, and the town was still dark. Outside, the air was very cold.

During the night, Ellen went to her room. The house was quiet. Mrs. Glynis built up the fire again with a little more wood. She heard Sarah breathing heavily.

On returning to the bedside, Mrs. Glynis saw that Sarah's breathing had stopped. Robert, now asleep, was still holding Sarah's hand. Mrs. Glynis picked up her other wrist to check for a pulse and felt nothing.

Sarah had slipped away. The snow lay thick upon the gardens and streets of Winchester. It was shortly before dawn

With a heavy heart, Mrs. Glynis took a candle to light her way down the darkened stairs to the parlor. No one was up, so she went quietly into the kitchen, where she lit a second candle.

In the bedroom upstairs, Robert awoke. He was still clasping Sarah's hand. It felt cold. He put his ear to her chest, and when he heard no heartbeat, he realized his wife was gone.

Robert gently placed Sarah's hand by her side and covered it with the blanket. Then he went to the window and looked out onto a white world of virgin snow. He suddenly felt old and very, very tired.

Poor Sarah—she had not wanted to come to America. Had he been responsible for her death? Would things have been different if they had remained in Wales?

Now his daughters would have to go forward without their mother, and he would have to go on without his wife.

When Mrs. Glynis returned to the bedside, she saw that Mr. Jones had discovered that his wife's breathing had stopped.

Although Robert could not imagine a new life without Sarah, a mingled sense of sadness and calm overtook him as he realized that her struggles were over. Sarah was finally at peace. "She's back in the Welsh valleys," he said aloud. "She's back home."

His face was wet with tears. Robert touched Sarah's cheek one last time, and then slowly drew the covers over her head. "Good-bye, my dear," he whispered. Quietly, to himself, he continued the Welsh song he had sung for Sarah. This time he did not stumble over the words. He remembered them clearly:

*Oeryw 'rrhew ac oerye 'reira*
(Cold is the frost, cold the snowfall)
*Oeryw 'rtyhebdânyn y gaeaf*
(Cold the house without fire in winter)
*Oeryw 'reglwyshebddimffeirad*
(Cold is the church without a vicar)
*Oeryw 'finnau heb fy 'nghariad.*
(Cold am I without my love.)

Downstairs, Mrs. Glynis put on the teakettle and got a cup from the cupboard. She fixed herself some hot tea. Then she built up the fire in the big coal and wood stove to heat the freezing kitchen. Soon it felt warmer, and Mrs. Glynis made herself a second cup of tea.

Outside, the morning sky grew lighter as a weak sun rose, and the snow continued to fall. Mrs. Glynis remained in the kitchen when Carrie entered it sometime later.

"I would have made your breakfast," Carrie said.

"I know, but I came down early to warm the

kitchen. Miss Sarah's gone. Mr. Jones is with her, and the girls are still asleep."

"I is sorry." Carrie shook her head. "She was a sad little person."

"Yes," said Mrs. Glynis. "She wasn't able to settle away from Wales."

"She just couldn't live here and be happy," Carrie agreed. "Bless her soul." Carrie wiped her eyes as she made porridge and coffee.

Mrs. Glynis watched the snow for a while until the sky grew lighter. "I must go home," she told Carrie as she put on her coat and bonnet. "But first, I'll send Dr. Mason to manage things here. Send Zack if you need me."

Mrs. Glynis went out of the kitchen into the cold, snowy morning. Meanwhile, the other occupants of the house slept.

Mrs. Taylor woke up late and hurried into the warm kitchen. "Good morning, Carrie," she greeted the freed slave. "You're up early."

"Yes, ma'am. Mrs. Glynis has gone for Dr. Mason. Miss Sarah died in the night."

"I was afraid she would," Mrs. Taylor replied, shaking her head sadly. "She was very unhappy, and she had no will to live. I feel so sorry for the girls. The world is a lonely place without your mother."

Dr. Mason arrived a shortly after the women finished their breakfast. He had walked over briskly in the fresh snow. Mrs. Taylor opened the door for him.

"Come in and have something hot to drink before you go upstairs," she offered.

"Mrs. Glynis said Miss Sarah died in the night. The Welsh lady is going to see the Episcopalian rector after she has rested. Reverend Cline, the Methodist minister, is out of town. What a capable woman, and such a good friend."

Mrs. Taylor led the doctor upstairs to Sarah's room. Robert was sitting at his wife's bedside. He did not speak or look up.

"Robert, I am so sorry to hear of Sarah's passing. My deepest condolences to you and to your girls," said Dr. Mason gently. Robert nodded in reply. Dr. Mason checked Sarah a final time for any signs of life and found none. Then all three of them left the room, closing Sarah's door until the funeral arrangement could be made.

After they were awakened and told the news, Annie and Ellen sat tearfully in the parlor of Mrs. Taylor's house. Robert sent word to Charlie to let him know what had happened, and then he sent Spotted Deer to New Town to get Monty. He thought it might help the girls to have the beloved pet near.

Spotted Deer rode Light Horse Harry the six miles to New Town to deliver the message. When the Indian lad arrived at Charlie's farm, he explained everything. "The Welsh ladies will be at Mrs. Taylor's trying to help the girls prepare for the burial," he told Charlie. "I came to pick up Monty and take him to Miss Annie and Miss Ellen."

Charlie nodded. "He will be a great comfort to them, especially Annie. Before you leave, come meet the Missus. Her name is Sally. She will want to give you something to eat while you have a rest. And tell me, how is Robert?"

"He is crushed. He feels as if it's his fault for bringing the family to America. Mrs. Glynis is making all the arrangements with the church for the service, since Mr. Robert is not well enough to make them himself."

"Tell Robert I can be there any time he needs me, and I'll come to the funeral."

At Charlie's farm, Monty came bounding across the field toward him as if he knew he was needed. He jumped up to greet Spotted Deer, who rubbed his ears.

"I suppose I had better get back now," said Spotted Deer. "I can carry the dog across the front of my saddle."

Soon after getting a drink of water, Spotted Deer

prepared to leave. He still had miles to travel back to Winchester, and with Monty on the front of the saddle, Light Horse Harry had extra weight to carry.

Charlie lifted Monty onto the saddle.

Spotted Deer turned his horse toward Winchester. Even carrying Monty, he moved at a good pace. The hound sat quietly and seemed to understand the urgency of the trip.

When Spotted Deer arrived at the boarding house with Monty, Mrs. Taylor answered the front door. With Carrie's help, Spotted Deer lowered the dog from Light Horse Harry's saddle. Carrie led Monty to the back parlor and knocked on the door. "I have a friend here to see you," she called. "He's just come from New Town."

Annie looked up as Monty bounded into her lap. He licked her face and barked his welcome, eager to tell her he loved her.

"Oh, Monty, how good to see you. I did miss you so very much!" She wiped tears from her eyes.

Ellen watched her sister play with the affectionate dog. "How big he's grown! That ugly stray is now a beautiful hound."

Meanwhile, Mrs. Glynis had gone to Christ Church to see the rector, who had welcomed her to his newly built church.

"Reverend Smith, I am a friend of the Jones family. Mrs. Jones died last night of typhoid fever, and we need to plan a private funeral for her. Her daughters are devastated, and her husband blames himself. They need some help and some comfort," Mrs. Glynis explained as she sat down in the chair Reverend Smith offered her.

"I'll arrange everything. There's a small plot available. I'll get the services and plot readied for tomorrow afternoon," the Reverend promised.

"There will be about a dozen people attending," Mrs. Glynis told him. "The family had only recently come here from Wales."

Mrs. Glynis then returned to the boarding house and knocked on the kitchen door. "Carrie, may I speak to you? Do you think we could have tea and cakes after the funeral tomorrow? Nothing fancy, just to finish the day with a little visitation."

Carrie looked as if she had been crying. "I's so glad you asked, 'cause I was goin' to ask you the same thing. I'd be happy to make tea and cakes. She was a nice little lady."

"That is true. But sad."

Carrie took out the magic teapot and washed it. Then she found some loose tea and several china cups. "These will do nicely," she said, looking at the display of china. "I'll make some cakes and send Zack to buy some from Mrs. Yoder down the road. This is her baking day. We can fix up a nice tea party."

Carrie sent Tommy over to the church for the linens, and when he got back, she starched and ironed them for the next day.

Meanwhile, Robert retreated to the cabin with Cyrus and Spotted Deer. He felt happier when he was busy on his land. The next day, at about midday, Charlie arrived. He was so dressed up that Annie didn't recognize him. As he stuck his head into Mrs. Taylor's back parlor, Monty jumped up and pawed at Charlie's good trousers.

"Hi, fella," Charlie greeted him. "You enjoying this high society?"

"Charlie, Charlie!" Annie cried. "How different you look all dressed up! Thank you for coming."

"I came up with the coach. I didn't want to ruin my good clothes. I wanted to be with your family today. Anyway, I had to see how Monty was behaving." Charlie sat on the settee between the sisters and took each girl's hand. "Just like old times seeing you both again."

"I am so happy you came," said Ellen. "Papa will be pleased to see you."

A little later, Mrs. Glynis came in and checked that everything was almost finished. Carrie had the linens done and the cakes were ready to serve. After lunch, Mrs. Glynis, Mrs. Taylor, and Carrie delivered the food to the church.

Just after, Annie and Ellen went upstairs to change, and Mrs. Glynis slipped away to do the same. Then Charlie escorted the ladies to the church. Robert was already there with Spotted Deer and Old Cyrus. Gwynn and the other Welsh ladies arrived, along with the Welsh couple, Yorweth and Blodwen, and Mrs. Taylor.

The service was simple. Reverend Smith said a homily, and they all sang some hymns that Sarah had liked. She was laid to rest in a land that was alien to her. The church wasn't even her own, but nevertheless, she was quietly buried in the adjoining cemetery. Robert appeared lost and sad, yet both Annie and Ellen knew that their mother would never have settled in America. She was not made of pioneer stuff, and she could not get used to life in America.

After the burial, the small group of mourners returned to the church parlor for tea and cakes.

"What a lovely reception," Annie told Carrie. "We appreciate all you have done."

"We liked Miss Sarah. She was a real fine lady," Carrie said. "A real fine lady in a country she didn't understand."

## OLD CYRUS'S SONG

"Robert is exhausted," Mrs. Taylor told Mrs. Glynis as the mourners gathered in the church's parlor. "He needs to go home. Cyrus, will you drive us?"

"Yes, of course," Old Cyrus agreed. He and Mrs. Taylor took Robert, along with Carrie's two boys, and left the church. The other guests remained for a visit and for the refreshments that Carrie and Mrs. Glynis prepared for the occasion. Robert shivered as Zack and Tommy helped him into the wagon.

Snow lay wet and heavy upon the ground. Tree branches cracked under the weight of the ice. Winchester appeared ugly, the gray streets filled with dirty snow, which was piled upon the roadsides to allow the horses to pass safely. The December light seemed eerie in the late afternoon.

"It's cold," Robert remarked as he sat in the wagon next to Old Cyrus. Tommy put a lap robe over his knees. "I feel lonesome and chilled this afternoon."

Cyrus drove through the slippery, snow-covered streets to Mrs. Taylor's house. Daniel Morgan and Light Horse Harry carefully picked their way as Cyrus skillfully guided them through the darkened evening.

Zack recognized Matt O'Reilly, the lamplighter, and waved to him. Every evening, Matt lit the whale oil lamps along the streets. He carried a long ladder to climb up on the tall poles. A glass globe was fitted over each burning lamp to reflect light upon the darkened road. Street lighting was new in Winchester, but Benjamin Franklin had introduced such lamps in Philadelphia some time ago. Matt O'Reilly took great pride in his street lamps and kept the wicks ready to light.

This evening, Zack waved and greeted the old man as the horses trotted past him. "Good evening to you all," Matt O'Reilly said. He waved back before he lit the street lamp. It cast a friendly glow across their path.

After a short drive, they came to Mrs. Taylor's boarding house. "Come in, Cyrus," Mrs. Taylor invited as he helped her down from the back seat. "I'll have some tea and hot chocolate ready in a few minutes. Put your horses in the stables behind the house. There are blankets in the end stall for Dan and Harry. You'll find oats there, too, and hay is in the loft."

Old Cyrus did as he was bidden after Zack and Tommy jumped down and gave Robert a hand to help him out of the wagon in the semi-darkness.

"Why didn't you boys stay for the refreshments? Robert asked Zack and Tommy.

"And have to talk to a lot of boring old ladies?" Zack replied. "I wanted to come home so Mr. Cyrus could tell us a story."

Once inside, Mrs. Taylor lit the big stove in the kitchen and added coal and some kindling to the dying embers. She put water on to boil for the tea and heated milk for hot chocolate.

"I'll take the coal scuttle and light the fires in the front and back parlors," Robert offered. He lifted the heavy scuttle and left the kitchen to build up the fires so the rooms would be warm when Annie, Ellen, and Carrie returned from the church.

Mrs. Taylor filled several whale oil lamps, which she lit and placed globes over the flames to reflect the light. As the evening deepened, the lamps threw ghostly shadows upon the kitchen walls, but the kitchen felt warm and friendly when the two boys and Cyrus entered it after taking care of the horses.

"Brrr," said Tommy, as he came in with his feet soaking wet. "It's cold and frosty this evening."

"Take off your shoes, boys," Mrs. Taylor instructed. "Put on these dry slippers. You'll soon warm up." She handed each of the shivering boys a pair of blue house shoes. "Now, set the chairs around the table, and I'll have your hot chocolate ready in a minute. Cyrus, do you want tea or chocolate?"

"I'll have the chocolate, ma'am," Cyrus replied. "I'll sweeten hit with a little moonshine. That'll make a grand hot toddy."

He took the spoon Tommy handed him and laced the cocoa with illegal whiskey. He offered none to the rest of the company; he jealously recorked the flask of precious liquid and put it in his pocket.

Robert returned with the scuttle after lighting the parlor fires and accepted a cup of tea.

"Have one of these little cakes to go with it," Mrs. Taylor told him. Then she passed the plate to Cyrus and the boys.

The atmosphere in the kitchen felt warm and companionable. "That's better," Zack said as he huddled beside the now-blazing hot stove. "Mr. Cyrus, can you tell us a story? An exciting story that's really true?"

Mrs. Taylor poured Robert some more tea as Cyrus cleared his throat and took a drink of his hot chocolate spiced with moonshine. He found his voice in good tone and, after clearing his throat a second time, began his tale.

"It was the first of June in 1781 when General Cornwallis captured a dispatch rider and learned that Governor Jefferson, Thomas Nelson, Patrick Henry, Benjamin Harrison, and Richard Henry Lee had left Richmond, which was where the Virginia capital had been moved from Williamsburg in 1780. Jefferson and the Virginia Assembly headed west to Charlottesville and to Monticello after the traitor Benedict Arnold and his British troops attacked Richmond." Old Cyrus stopped to take another drink of his hot toddy.

"Did I ever tell you the story of Jack Jouett and how he rescued Thomas Jefferson from Banastre Tarleton and his 'green coats'? That's what we called the British cavalry, because they wore green jackets. It was a difficult rescue, since Mr. Jefferson had no sense of time. Who else would wait for his horse to be re-shod before he got on him to escape? The British cavalry were riding up one side of Monticello while Mr. Jefferson mounted his horse and started down the mountain on the other side! Some folks, I tell you—and smart folks, too—just are blindsided by danger when minutes count, when folks need to leave or they'll be captured.

"Jack Jouett, a young man of about twenty-six who was a captain in the Virginia militia, happened to be asleep in the yard of the Cuckoo Tavern in Louisa County when he was awakened by the tramp of horses' hooves. Hit was Tarleton's men comin' by on their way to Louisa Courthouse, which was a few miles down the road. The British planned to capture Mr. Jefferson and other members of the Virginia Legislature at Monticello. Jack's father owned Swan's Tavern near Charlottesville, as well as a farm in Louisa County, which supplied food for the American troops under Nathanael Greene in North Carolina.

"Jack knowed all the shortcuts over the Old Mountain Road, which was really a rough path through the Blue Ridge. He had a stout horse named Bob White. Bob was part thoroughbred and could outrace most horses. He also had the stamina to make the long climb up to Monticello.

"It was a moon-bright night, with a full moon shining almost like day. Jack mounted Bob, and they scrambled up the hillside and skirted the British encampment with only a hooty-owl to guide their route through the piney woods. The old barn owl seemed to know the importance of Jack's mission, and he flew ahead of them up the mountain. Jack reckoned it was nearly midnight when he left Cuckoo Tavern, and it was a good forty miles up in the mountains to Monticello.

"Meanwhile, Colonel Tarleton and his troops found eleven wagons headed south to carry supplies to General Greene in North Carolina. The British burned the wagons, and stopped at Boswell's Tavern near Louisa Courthouse for three hours to rest their horses and to celebrate. Those three hours allowed Jack and Bob White to make the steep climb and to reach Monticello in the wee hours of the morning.

"Some peoples haven't a bit of sense. Mr. Jefferson is one of them. He's blindsided like some mules. Here the British cavalry is coming to arrest him, and Mr. Jefferson hadn't the sense to get on his horse and run. No, sir, there he is early in the morning talking to his gardener. Finally, he sent his family off to a neighboring plantation fourteen miles away, but still Mr. Jefferson didn't leave. He and the Virginia Assembly members, who were guests at Monticello, had to eat breakfast! Mr. Jefferson even found time to offer Jack Jouett a glass of good Madeira wine!

"The British were nearly at his doorstep before Mr. Jefferson finished gathering up state papers and a-waiting for his horse to be re-shod. The British cavalrymen were crossing the lawn of Monticello before Jefferson finally mounted his horse and rode down the mountain trails toward Charlottesville. Jack left shortly before to warn his family at Swan's Tavern.

"Mr. Jefferson got away, but other members of the Virginia Assembly were not as lucky. The British caught seven of them, including Daniel Boone. The important members, such as Patrick Henry, Thomas Nelson, who became the next governor, Benjamin Harrison, and Richard Henry Lee escaped. But no thanks to Mr. Jefferson. He took all of God's sweet time to leave Monticello. He was as slow as a water turtle crawling on his belly across the land. It was lucky that Mr. Jefferson's horses knowed the trails through the woods down from Monticello to Charlottesville and over to Staunton, about thirty-five miles away, where the members of the legislature agreed to meet. Mr. Jefferson was a stubborn old cuss. He had red hair, and that maybe accounts for it."

"So, Mr. Jefferson got away?" Zack interrupted, excited by the story. "Colonel Tarleton was nobody to fool with, although it was another officer who actually came to arrest the Virginia Assembly at Monticello."

"How do you know that?" Old Cyrus asked. "Jefferson was so smart he was stupid. To wait for your horse to be re-shod doesn't scow with the smarts a governor of Virginia should possess."

"What's 'scow' mean?" Tommy asked Cyrus. "I never heard that word."

"To scow is for the plough to dig into the earth and break it open. If a plough doesn't scow, it just slides over the top and doesn't break into the earth. It doesn't open the furrows so the seeds can be planted. It's a farmer's word. That's why city folks like you and Zack have never heard of it.

"After Mr. Jefferson toasted Jack with his good Madeira wine," Old Cyrus continued, "Jack left Monticello to warn the Assembly members who were staying at Swan's Tavern. The men staying there did not dilly-dally, but jumped up and got away in time. Jack knew the trails and cattle paths through the mountains, and he took the men through these hidden pathways toward Staunton. As I said, seven members of the legislature were captured, and among them was Daniel Boone."

Old Cyrus stopped to lace a second cup of chocolate with moonshine. Again, he didn't offer anyone else a drop of his precious drink, but recorked the flask and secured it in his boot.

"I must keep my whistle clear for more storytelling," Old Cyrus explained. He began to hum, and after he found his voice in good repair, he sang this song:

> *There was a clever man whose name was Jack Jouett*
> *Who fell asleep at the Cuckoo Tavern*
> *When Tarleton and his 'green coats' came riding by*
> *Jack heard them boastfully cry,*
> *'We're off to capture Jefferson!'*
> *Tarleton and his men spent*
> *Three hours at Boswell's Inn*
> *Near Louisa Courthouse*
> *Drinking and bragging*
> *About the wagons they captured*
> *That night and set aflame.*
> *The 'jollification' went on*
> *Until two hours in the morn.*
> *When they left, it was nearly dawn.*
>
> *But Jack Jouett was on his way*
> *Long before the break of day.*
> *He rode his horse, Bob White*
> *Forty rough miles*
> *In the bright moonlight*
> *And got to Monticello long before day*
> *To hurry Mr. Jefferson on his way.*

"That poem doesn't rhyme," Zack objected as Cyrus finished his tale about Jack Jouett and Thomas Jefferson.

"You axed me to tell you a story about something real. That's as real as I can make it. Every word is true. You said nothing about rhymin'." Cyrus looked hurt. "You can't satisfy anyone these days. Mrs. Taylor, give me another dose of that hot chocolate. It makes a grand toddy." Cyrus felt warm and tingling. "Didn't you appreciate my story and poem?" He looked to Mrs. Taylor for comfort, since his best audience had failed him.

"It's a very fine tale," she told Cyrus as she filled

his cup with hot chocolate.

"Later, I met Jack Jouett," Old Cyrus continued. "He was a pleasant sort of fellow and a real hero. Without his quick thinking, Jefferson and the whole legislature would have been captured," Cyrus settled back into the easy chair, feeling satisfied with both his hot toddy and his storytelling.

## VISITORS

Charlie stayed over an extra day after Sarah's funeral so that he could visit Robert's farm. There was snow in the mountains. The cabin was covered with frozen crystals that glistened in the sunlight.

"You got a nice place here," Charlie remarked, as he and Robert walked over the farm. "It's good fertile land."

"Yes. With Cyrus and Spotted Deer's help, it should be profitable once we get started." Robert watched Monty run through the snow after a squirrel. "We should do well."

A few days later, Ellen and Annie approached their father. "Papa," said Ellen, "we would like to stay in town. Annie is continuing her training to teach, and Dr. Mason has asked me to be an assistant in his office. That will mean I'm earning wages. You take Monty out to the farm with you, and we'll come on the weekends," she continued. "The farm is beautiful, but we enjoy being part of the community," Ellen told him. "Charlie said he would come up often and hunt with you and Monty. And with Spotted Deer and Old Cyrus on hand, you won't be alone."

Robert had known this day would come. His wife's death had only hastened it, and he understood. He gave his daughters his blessing and arranged for their training. He felt happiest on the farm, with Old Cyrus and Spotted Deer for companionship.

The snow lay deep on the ground that winter, so the girls could not come on the weekends. Slowly, however, Robert felt at home in Virginia. Old Cyrus and Spotted Deer worked on the cabin's interior, and gradually it became less rustic and began to look like a real house. Mrs. Glynis had a local weaver make a coverlet for Robert's bedroom. Old Cyrus constructed a mantelpiece and shutters to keep out the wind.

March arrived, bringing with it an early spring.

Robert's house became an attractive place to visit, and the girls came often to see their father.

By spring, the cabin was nearly finished and most of the furniture had been made. The barn was almost complete, and as the season progressed, new calves appeared in the fields. Robert dabbled in fishing once the ice broke and the weather turned warm.

"Mr. Robert, you can't fish in the winter," Old Cyrus had told him.

"Yes, I know," Robert would reply, and continued to fish sitting on the bank or wading in the cold mountain stream.

The calves also took a lot of Robert's time and attention. Annie named one of them "Rambeau," which was how she imagined the French might spell the word "rambunctious."

"Papa, come back into town this weekend," Annie begged her father. "Mrs. Glynis has been asking for you."

"How is the dear lady?" Robert inquired. "She was such a great help, but I can't keep begging her for favors."

"No," said Annie. "But you can come into town for a visit every now and then."

"Yes, but I need to work with Old Cyrus until we get the barn finished and the farm is stocked with sheep and chickens," Robert said. "Rambeau needs watching because he gets into trouble. I don't want Mrs. Glynis to think I am a lazy oaf who does nothing except fish."

"She doesn't feel that way," Annie told him. "She's just wondering what makes you so busy that you can't come into town."

"There's plenty to do. Why doesn't Mrs. Glynis ride out here with you next weekend?" Robert suggested. "I'd like her to see the farm. There are animals in the barn, and a house with furniture and spring water. It's my home now."

Annie realized that her father's reluctance to visit

Winchester was not because he didn't like the people there, but because the thought of Sarah's death was still painful to him. In the country, where she'd never visited, her spirit haunted him less, but Mrs. Taylor's home brought back too many memories that Robert wished to avoid.

As winter snow gave way to spring, Robert found he needed supplies. Rambeau was almost a month old and seemed less prone to getting into trouble. He followed Robert around the barnyard like a puppy. The cattle were contained in a pasture by strong board fences and the barn was finished, so Robert couldn't avoid a visit to town.

"We must make a trip to Winchester," Old Cyrus insisted, as he got out the harness and cleaned it. He also greased the axles on the wagon. "We need to get some seed for planting and buy more chickens."

"Why can't Annie or Ellen bring some out?" Robert protested.

"Robert, Annie can't carry on Paint all the things we need. We'll have to take the wagon and both Daniel Morgan and Light Horse Harry Lee. Maybe we can bring Mrs. Glynis back if we have the wagon. It's easier than riding horseback. I'm sure she would like to see what we have accomplished."

Robert allowed the matter to drop until Annie rode out a week later.

"Papa, Mrs. Glynis would like to come and see the farm. I told her how much you, Spotted Deer, and Old Cyrus have done. She'd like to come out with her sister, Miss Gwynn, and see the place."

"Would she?" Robert asked.

"Yes, she would." Annie was not going to be put off. "She asked me only yesterday when she and Miss Gwynn might come for a visit."

"Oh, all right—but why is she so interested?" Robert asked his daughter. "It's only a half-made farm."

"Because she's interested in American life, and

your farm is part of American life." Annie grew impatient as they sat in the cabin by the hearth and drank their tea. "Oh, Monty." She patted the brown hound. "Some folks could drive you crazy."

The next Saturday morning, Mrs. Glynis and Miss Gwynn prepared to drive out with Dr. Mason's team and carriage to visit Robert. Dr. Mason had asked Golden Eagle to bring them in style. The Indian groom put red ribbons in the horses' manes and used the best harness, which he had cleaned for the occasion. The black hunter, Lafayette, was accompanied by another horse, Marcus. Marcus was just as dark, except for a white star on his forehead.

At mid-morning, Golden Eagle brought the team to the Welsh ladies' front door, ready to make the drive to the farm. Annie, mounted on Paint, planned to accompany them.

"How do you like my new riding habit, Golden Eagle?" she inquired. "A friend at her church gave it to Mrs. Mason, and it was just my size."

"It's grand, Miss Annie," Golden Eagle replied as they waited for Mrs. Glynis and Miss Gwynn. "You will have to learn to ride sidesaddle with that getup. No more riding astride."

Mrs. Glynis and Miss Gwynn appeared almost immediately, dressed in country clothes and heavy shoes. It was late March, but still cold, so Golden Eagle drove an enclosed carriage and brought a lap robe to protect the ladies from the wind.

"Good morning, Mrs. Glynis, Miss Gwynn," Annie greeted the sisters. "We have a lovely morning for our trip to the farm."

"Is Mr. Jones expecting us?" Mrs. Glynis asked. "Or will this be a surprise?"

"No, no," Annie hastened to reply. "He knows you are coming this morning. I wanted him to come into town, but he was anxious for you to see the farm. He's gone crazy over fishing. He says it's good for his brains."

Golden Eagle helped the ladies into the carriage and covered their legs with the heavy blue lap robe. Then he climbed onto his seat and clucked to Marcus and Lafayette to walk on. Annie rode in front of them on Paint. She looked rather elegant in her hand-me-down riding habit and sat sidesaddle until they reached the stony road to the mountains.

"You look very fashionable," Mrs. Glynis remarked.

"It's rather nice, don't you think, and it fits me. Well, it almost fits me." Annie walked Paint down Piccadilly Street and then turned west toward the mountains.

"Brrr," said Miss Gwynn. "It's cold this morning. My nose is frozen." She covered her face with her scarf.

"You look like an outlaw," Annie laughed. "Father will think you've come to rob him."

They left Winchester and turned onto the stony road toward the Allegheny Mountains. Once the town was behind them, Annie wanted to ride astride. With Mrs. Glynis and Miss Gwynn behind her in the carriage, however, she decided she needed to keep up her appearance as an accomplished horsewoman and continued to ride sidesaddle.

"You look well," Golden Eagle said approvingly. "Like a real lady."

"It's not very comfortable, but I guess I can manage it for a while," Annie complained.

"What a beautiful area," Miss Gwynn said. "It's really a different world back here in the mountains."

"Yes," Golden Eagle replied as he guided the horses. "It's wonderful when the white dogwoods bloom and the redbud trees make the woods look pink. We grow a lot of apples here in the Shenandoah Valley. It's a pink-and-white fairyland when the fruit trees are in bloom."

"How long will it take for us to reach the farm?" Miss Gwynn inquired.

"About an hour, if all goes well. Sometimes we meet other horses and riders on the road. It's difficult to pass them with two horses and a carriage. There are lay-bys we have to go on to allow the other horses and wagons to pass. It's still early, so we should be all right for other traffic."

"When was Mr. Jones last in Winchester?" Mrs. Glynis asked.

Annie turned Paint around so she could walk beside the carriage and talk to the ladies as they went along. "Old Cyrus and Spotted Deer came in for supplies this past week, but Papa didn't join them. He likes to fish and sit by in the creek, so he stayed at the farm." She didn't explain that her father avoided going because he found Winchester full of memories that were too fresh and too painful for him to encounter.

"Well, we've come to see him," Mrs. Glynis said. "I brought a home-cooked lunch so we can have a little party. I'm looking forward to exploring the farm."

After an hour's drive, they reached the ridge that overlooked the land grant, and Golden Eagle skillfully brought the carriage down the stony road toward the new barn. Old Cyrus sat under the budding trees on a homemade stool. He held his unlit pipe in his mouth as he repaired a broken bridle. His dog, Danny, lay at his feet.

Spotted Deer saw the visitors from afar. "Hello there!" he shouted to them, waving. "Welcome to Mr. Robert's farm. Come on down."

Since the last 500 yards were rocky and precipitous, Golden Eagle was forced to take care of his team, but Annie waved back.

"Hello, Cyrus, Spotted Deer! We have come for a visit and have brought you some lunch."

Spotted Deer ran up the rocky path to greet the

visitors. "Come on down," he said. "Mr. Robert's gone fishing up the creek a-ways. I'll go tell him you're here. Miss Annie, don't you look grand in your new riding habit? You're riding sidesaddle! Well, now," Spotted Deer remarked, impressed.

"I don't like it," Annie replied. "But with the ladies coming and the new outfit, I thought I'd better try to be a proper horsewoman."

"You look quite the lady," Old Cyrus said as he gained the path and led the carriage horses down to the barn.

Robert sat beside the creek fishing. As he observed the carriage and horses coming down from the ridge, he realized that visitors had arrived. "Is that Mrs. Glynis and her sister?" he asked himself. "It's quite a lovely carriage with a matched pair of black horses. I'd better go and see." He reeled in his line and laid his rod against a tree, then walked down the creek toward the barn with Monty at his heels.

"Hello, Mr. Jones," Mrs. Glynis called. "Here we are, at last."

"Hello, Mrs. Glynis! So glad you could come." Robert strode up to the barn to greet her. "And Miss Gwynn, too!" he exclaimed, clearly pleased to have so many visitors.

"The ladies have brought you a home-cooked meal!" Annie rode Paint down the path toward him. "This is a festival day, Papa."

"I believe it. It must be, with all this company, and the ladies' arrival in a carriage," Robert said as he helped the visitors step down.

Then he spoke to Ellen. "Hello, my dear."

"Hello, Papa." She jumped from the carriage and embraced him."

"Let me take the horses," Old Cyrus offered. "I'll look after them. Miss Annie, can you get off in all that fancy rig-out you've got on?"

Spotted Deer held Paint while Annie dismounted. Robert came into the barn while she rearranged her skirts and took off her fancy hat. "Hello, Papa," she greeted him. "How are you?"

"I've been enjoying my fishing," Robert said. "Come see our Leicester Longwool sheep and our Dominique chickens." He led the ladies out of the barn toward a newly built chicken coop and run. "We have fifty hens, and Cyrus sells our eggs at the farmers' market. So it's a real farm," Robert told them proudly. "We got some seed corn last week to plant as soon as the frost is gone."

"My goodness," said Mrs. Glynis, admiring the new sheep and chickens. "What a lot of work you've done."

"Yes," Old Cyrus added proudly. "We've got the cabin furnished and a spring to carry water from. I built a gate, and Spotted Deer made some of the furniture."

"Come on down to the cabin," Robert invited. "Let me carry your lunch. What a treat to have a home-cooked meal!"

"It's so lovely here," Mrs. Glynis remarked as they made their way down the path toward the newly finished cabin. Smoke rose from the chimney.

"Is it warm enough in here?" Spotted Deer asked the visitors as they entered the cabin to find a neatly arranged home. There was one large room with a central fireplace and a loft. On the left side, Annie saw Robert's bedroom. Old Cyrus usually slept by the fireplace and Spotted Deer claimed the loft when they were at the farm. The two dogs slept on clean straw pallets.

The furniture, although handmade, was of an old European style. Old Cyrus was a good craftsman and had taught Spotted Deer the art of making furniture, and now he was teaching Robert.

"How wonderful," said Mrs. Glynis. She appeared greatly surprised by the quality of the furnishings in the cabin. "What a cozy home you have, Mr. Jones!"

"We've worked on it, and Cyrus has even taught me how to make a three-legged stool," Robert said with a laugh. "We found the quilts and curtains at the farmers' market. There's a German woman there, Mrs. Yoder, who makes them. She made each of us a patchwork quilt, and she insisted we have the curtains."

Annie saw Monty in the pasture. "Look, Papa, he's herding the sheep!"

"Oh, yes," Robert replied. "Cyrus has turned him into a herding dog. He and Danny bring the sheep into the barn every evening and take them out in the morning. Herding dogs are a necessity. The Leicester sheep hate being herded, and they stand and face Monty and Danny then slowly back into the pasture."

Mrs. Glynis laughed. "He's a jack-of-all-trades, that Monty. By the way, have you heard from Charlie Smithson recently?"

"Yes," replied Robert. "Spotted Deer rode down to New Town to attend the sheep sales and saw Charlie. He's doing all right. He misses Monty. Charlie plans to come to Winchester in April for the cattle sales. I hope to see him then."

Spotted Deer put the heavy pot of Mrs. Glynis' stew on the fire to warm it. Then he started some water to boil for their tea. As he worked, Mrs. Glynis and Miss Gwynn placed a blue-and-white cloth on the table and arranged the plates, cutlery, and napkins they brought. Miss Gwynn put chairs and stools around the table for seven people while Spotted Deer made tea. Then Mrs. Glynis called everyone to come to the table for dinner.

"What an elegant table you set, Mrs. Glynis," Robert said with appreciation. "I haven't sat down to a meal like this since I left Mrs. Taylor's boarding house."

Mrs. Glynis smiled at the compliment and felt especially pleased that Robert appreciated her hard work.

Everyone found a place. Mrs. Glynis served, and Spotted Deer brought the kettle and poured out the tea. Old Cyrus carried butter and milk in from the springhouse, then they all sat down together and ate a hearty lunch. Nobody spoke while they ate the stew and bread that Mrs. Glynis had made the previous day. The party continued through the dessert of little cakes Miss Gwynn brought for the occasion.

"What a wonderful dinner!" said a delighted Robert. "I can't eat another mouthful. I'm stuffed."

"That was a treat," Old Cyrus agreed. "What a good cook you are, Mrs. Glynis."

Spotted Deer offered them a final cup of tea before he gathered up the plates and cutlery to wash.

"I hate to remind you, but it's time you got ready to leave for Winchester," said Old Cyrus as the sun appeared low in the sky. "It will be dark soon, and it's best you get on your way out of the mountains."

Quickly, Spotted Deer gathered up the clean dishes and packed them into Mrs. Glynis' white oak basket. Golden Eagle and Old Cyrus harnessed the horses and hitched them to the carriage. Annie struggled into her skirt to mount Paint, and soon they were ready to leave. Old Cyrus led Marcus and Lafayette up to the ridge and waved the visitors good-bye.

"That was fun," Spotted Deer told Annie as he led her pony onto the ridge above the stream.

"Yes, it was" Annie agreed. "And Papa looked really happy again. It's the first time I've heard him laugh since Mother died."

"That's good news," Spotted Deer said as he let go of Paint's bridle. He watched Annie follow behind the carriage that would take the visitors back to Winchester.

## OLD CYRUS AND HIS SHEEP

In late March, Charlie drove to Winchester for another stock sale, and afterward, he came again to visit Robert on his farm. Old Cyrus puffed up the hillside, breathless, to meet him and led the horses down from the ridge to the barn.

"How are those Leicester rams treating you?" Charlie asked as he climbed out of the wagon drawn by Jefferson and Madison.

"They's a right pain in my neck," Old Cyrus told him. "Two rams and ten ewes. Nobody needs a dozen crazy sheep! Let me take your horses into the upper part of the barn and unhitch them."

Charlie and Cyrus worked together to settle the horses. Then they walked beside the stream on their way to the cabin. "What are the sheep like now that you've gotten to know them?" Charlie asked, curious.

"Cornwallis is full of fight. I'm still thanking our lucky stars that he has no horns."

"I've been thinking, Cyrus," said Charlie, with a slight smile. He was amused by the whole affair with the rams and their ridiculous names. "Why not Francis Marion, the Swamp Fox, or 'Gamecock' Sumter? They're better names."

"Not for that ram. He's no American. He's arrogant and stubborn, just like Cornwallis." Cyrus spit on the ground in disgust. "As for the second ram, Banastre Tarleton—he'll butt the mischief out of anyone who comes near him. If we've spent all day a-building a board fence, those rams can knock it down in a minute."

"You don't like the sheep business, I take it." Charlie laughed as they stopped to skip flat stones across the swift-flowing stream.

"Not one tittle," Cyrus declared. "Why don't you take those rams down to New Town? I never want to see another sheep! Who was that young man with the funny name that we bought them from? Do you know him?"

"He was on the wagon train," Charlie explained. "He and his wife came from Wales like Robert and Sarah. Yorweth is the man's name, and Blodwen is his wife's. You'll see, Cyrus, in a few years more English purebred sheep will be imported."

"Well, you take those rams to New Town and let them knock down your board fences. Even Monty can't control those fellows, and he's the best herding dog in the valley. Let the Welsh keep their unruly animals and their strange-sounding names." Old Cyrus skipped another flat stone across the stream. "I had enough of these sheep, and I don't wish to have any more."

Charlie laughed and skipped his final stone. "Just wait, Cyrus. One day you'll be proud of Shenandoah Valley animals. And these sheep aren't really from Wales; they're from Leicester in England."

"Charlie, maybe what you say is true, but please deliver me from Welsh sheep!"

# TRAVELERS

As the spring came and the world burst into blossom and birdsong, Annie attended classes to become a teacher. She hoped to teach music as an extra course. Ellen tended to patients with Dr. Mason.

One afternoon, Annie, accompanied by Mrs. Glynis, saw a strange instrument displayed in a shop in Winchester. She vaguely remembered Johnny playing something similar on their long journey to Virginia. She asked the German proprietor what it was.

"It's called a 'zitter' in German, a dulcimer in English," Mr. Hartzog told her.

"I saw a boy playing one once," said Annie. "I remember he played it by plucking the strings with his fingers."

"You can also play it with a goose or turkey feather," Mr. Hartzog replied. "This instrument was made here in our mountains from native wood. You'll find these instruments wherever the Germans have settled throughout the valley. The Scots-Irish are now taking them up because they can play on the dulcimer the same tunes they play on the bagpipes—with a lot less trouble. It takes much less wind."

Annie touched the tear-shaped box. It was partly covered by a second, thinner box, and had frets and five strings for playing.

"Look, Miss, I'll show you how it works. It has a nice tone. The word 'dulcimer' means 'sweet music,' and so it has." Mr. Hartzog took up the dulcimer and placed it on his lap. Then he took a plucked turkey feather and began to strum the strange-looking instrument.

"I like the sound," said Annie. "Do you think I could learn to play it?"

"Yes, of course, Miss," the German proprietor answered. "Can you come down in the late afternoons? My wife can teach you the basic fingerings."

"Yes, that would be wonderful! Can I play Welsh folk songs on the dulcimer?" Annie wanted to know. "I don't play bagpipes."

"Yes, of course," Mr. Hartzog assured her. "You can play all sorts of music."

Annie had been teaching, and she'd earned a little money of her own. "I'd like to buy it," she said. "What time shall I come for my lesson? I could leave the dulcimer here for now, and return later this afternoon."

Annie felt delighted because she had always wanted to learn to play a mountain instrument. Since her mother's death, she had at times felt overwhelmed by sadness, and she thought that playing and singing old Welsh tunes might help her feel better when those sad feelings came.

Several days later, Charlie came to visit Winchester bearing exciting news for Annie and Ellen. "There's going to be a dance at my neighbor's in April after Easter," he said. "Maybe you can come down for it and stay with my wife and me at our farm."

"Maybe Mrs. Glynis and her sister could come as well," Annie suggested.

So it was arranged that Mrs. Glynis and Miss Gwynn would drive down in the carriage and chaperone Annie and Ellen at the dance. Dr. Mason heard about their outing, and he agreed to let them use his carriage and horses. Mrs. Mason had a pony and cart the doctor could use for his rounds and in case of a medical emergency.

Annie, meanwhile, taught herself the rudiments of dulcimer playing. She rode Paint to try to perfect her horse riding. She still preferred riding astride, but Major Skinner, a retired cavalryman who took an interest and worked with her, encouraged her to ride in the sidesaddle.

"It's awkward," Annie protested. "It's restricting, with all that skirt and the tall hat with veils. I hate it."

"It's very elegant," the Major told her. "A lady must

ride sidesaddle, my dear."

Annie often went with Mrs. Glynis to her school to observe her teaching methods. She also spent time with Miss Gwynn and the other teacher, Miss Mary, to watch them handle their classes. Several grades were grouped together in one room, and Miss Gwynn juggled various subjects.

Annie found it confusing to teach in a one-room school with children of various ages and abilities. She preferred to work individually, and began to teach a ten-year-old boy named Dolf. His name was really Adolphus McMillan, but 'Dolf' was easier. He had been ill with measles and was behind in his lessons.

"He's really a great little boy," Annie told her sister. "I find he's making good progress in spite of my lack of experience in teaching."

"Well, I seem to be making almost no progress on the dulcimer," Annie complained. "It's not easy. I much prefer playing the fiddle. That I can do with some skill."

Two weeks later, early on a Friday afternoon, Charlie came back into town on horseback. He went to Mrs. Taylor's looking for Annie and Ellen.

"Charlie, how nice to see you," said Mrs. Taylor. "I hear this Saturday is the dance in New Town. Annie and Ellen can talk of nothing else. What brings you here today?"

"I came for the stock sales," Charlie explained. "And I wanted to say hello to the girls."

"I'll call Annie," said Mrs. Taylor. "She's upstairs playing her dulcimer. She's about to drive herself and the rest of us crazy with it."

"I have a friend in New Town who plays the dulcimer and can give her an extra lesson while she's visiting," Charlie said. "But Annie's pretty good at the fiddle, I understand."

"Yes, she is," agreed Mrs. Taylor. "If she'd just

play the fiddle, we'd all be happier." As she started upstairs, she heard the sound of a dulcimer coming from Annie's room.

Carrie, hearing voices coming from the parlor, stuck her head around the kitchen door. "Oh, Mr. Charlie!" she cried, startled to see him. "I didn't know you were here."

"I've come for the stock sales, and to get Miss Annie and Miss Ellen for the dance we're having in New Town this coming weekend."

"Would you like something cold to drink?" Carrie offered.

Mrs. Glynis and Miss Gwynn were ready to leave Winchester for New Town at mid-afternoon. They were to ride in the carriage with Ellen while Annie rode Paint the six miles to New Town. It was straight down Valley Road, which had been recently resurfaced and repaired.

Golden Eagle arrived at Mrs. Taylor's house to pick up Annie and Ellen late. The carriage could accommodate three passengers and the coachmen with comfort.

Although she had practiced riding in the sidesaddle and the Major had given her a few lessons, Annie still disliked it. Since the trip to New Town for a dance required her to act like a lady, however, she mounted Paint with a new determination.

"You look really grand," Charlie encouraged her as she settled herself into the saddle.

"Oh, Charlie, how I long for the days when I rode Adams with no restrictions! I feel like a baked potato all squinched into a shell."

Charlie laughed. "That's a good way of expressing it! Good afternoon, Mrs. Glynis, Miss Gwynn."

"Good afternoon," the ladies replied, as Ellen stepped into the carriage and placed Annie's dulcimer on the seat next to her.

## CHARLIE'S FARM

Charlie, astride Madison, led the party south down Valley Road.

"What beautiful farm country!" declared Mrs. Glynis, impressed by the Shenandoah Valley. "This is really a rich and prosperous land."

"Yes, it is beautiful," agreed Miss Gwynn. "Are the farms owned by Germans or by the Scots-Irish?"

"Both," Charlie told her. "The Scots-Irish live in clusters, but the Germans predominate in the Valley."

After a half hour, Charlie turned off Valley Road onto a dirt lane.

"Look over there," he said, pointing to an attractive dwelling. "That is our house, and beyond it is the barn. My son, James, has been very excited about your coming. I thought he'd be here to meet us."

The farm looked prosperous with its numerous outbuildings. In addition to the barn and the house, there was a corncrib, a dairy, a smokehouse, a springhouse, an outside kitchen made of brick, and a blacksmith's forge. Charlie and his fellow smiths sold iron cut nails, which were a recent invention and in great demand.

Charlie hardly finished speaking when a boy of sixteen appeared. He had inherited Charlie's red hair, and a thousand freckles covered his face. He ran down the road to meet them.

"Papa," James shouted, "have you brought our visitors?" Behind James trotted an old brown and white hound dog, its long ears flapping when it ran to greet Charlie at the farm lane.

"That's Prince," Charlie explained to the visitors, and the old dog barked his delight to see them.

"Papa," said James, out of breath. "What took you so long? Hello, Miss Annie—hello, Miss Ellen. How's Monty?"

"He's turned into a herding dog for Papa's sheep," Annie replied. "Would you believe it?"

"This is Mrs. Glynis and her sister, Miss Gwynn," said Charlie. "Ladies, this is my son, James." Charlie took his foot out of the left stirrup to allow James to swing up onto the horse behind his father. "We'll give you a lift home," he said, "but Prince will have to walk."

"Golden Eagle, bring the carriage up the farm road into the barn. I have stabling, but there is a small paddock next to the barn if you prefer. My horses are turned out in another field," Charlie said. "There's a cabin behind the barn you can use."

As the horses pulled up the hill toward the barn, Charlie's wife, Sally, alerted by Prince's barking, came down the farm lane to greet her guests.

Prince ran to her and barked again to tell her that their visitors had arrived.

"Yes, Prince," she said, patting the dog's head. "Isn't it exciting?"

"Hello, Mrs. Smithson," Annie said, waving. She couldn't remember her hostess's first name because Charlie always simply referred to her as 'my wife.' "We are excited to be here and to meet you. I always think of you as "Mrs. Charlie." I'm Annie, these are the ladies from Wales, Mrs. Glynis and Miss Gwynn, and my sister, Ellen."

"Hello, everyone! Welcome to Spring Creek Farm. We're happy you're here! Come inside for some refreshment."

Golden Eagle brought the horses and carriage to a halt and jumped down to help the ladies.

"I'll hold your horses' heads," said Charlie, sliding off Madison and leaving James to ride the horse into the field where Jefferson, Adams, and Washington grazed.

Prince followed James and Madison to the pasture. Mrs. Charlie took her visitors to the house for something to eat. Charlie helped Golden Eagle with Marcus, Lafayette, and Paint.

"I've prepared some bread and apple butter made with apples from our own trees. And surely you'll have a cup of tea?" Mrs. Charlie offered.

"That would be grand," said Annie.

After the visitors took turns at the washing sink, Mrs. Charlie brought them into the house's dining area, which had its own fireplace and blue-and-white-checkered curtains. The main kitchen was in a separate stone building a good ways behind the house. Sally had an artist's sense of color, and the dining room was decorated with a certain amount of style. A warm fire greeted them.

"What a lovely room!" exclaimed Mrs. Glynis. "It looks especially cheerful with the brightly colored curtains and the Valley furniture."

"Thank you," said Mrs. Charlie. "The chairs and table were made by local craftsmen. My husband made the iron grate and the fire tools, as well as the wall sconces for the candles. Do sit down," she said, pointing to the harvest table with its comfortable chairs. "The tea is ready, and the bread and apple butter are laid out."

Mrs. Glynis and Miss Gwynn sat down while Ellen and Annie helped their hostess pass around the teacups.

James appeared a few minutes later. "Papa's helping Golden Eagle to unharness the carriage horses," he explained to his mother. "I brought Miss Annie's dulcimer up. Papa said she might need it."

"Can you play it?" Mrs. Charlie inquired of Annie.

"Not very well," Annie replied. "I'm learning slowly. It's a mixed-up instrument. It's rather like the Austrian zither from the Tyrol, on which the strings pass over the body without a neck. I like the sound of the dulcimer, though. I can play some of the old bagpipe music on it."

"Dulcimers have a pretty sound," Mrs. Charlie agreed as she passed the bread plate to James.

"Thank you," Mrs. Glynis said as she accepted another cup of tea.

"I can see Maria coming," said Mrs. Charlie. "She helps me in the dairy."

Across the field walked a young girl, limping. She carried two large milk pails, which she left in the springhouse before she came into the kitchen

"Does she live here?" Ellen asked.

"No, she lives in the Presbyterian manse," Mrs. Charlie told her. "She was raised by the minister, Rev. McPherson, and his wife after Maria was found abandoned on their doorstep."

"That's sad," said Miss Gwynn. "Did they ever find out who left her?"

"No," replied Mrs. Charlie. "But a wagon train had passed through town that morning going to the German Moravian settlement at Salem in North Carolina. We think someone on the wagon train must have left her."

"How old was she?" Mrs. Glynis inquired.

"Oh, just a baby, not yet a year old," Mrs. Charlie replied. "She was crippled and sickly. The mother probably was afraid she wouldn't make the trip, so she left Maria at the minister's door here."

Maria entered the dining area and came in carrying a small milk can. "Hello, Miss Sally. I brought you some milk for your visitors," she said. "The larger cans are in the springhouse, and I churned some butter this morning."

"Maria, I want you to meet my guests from Wales—Mrs. Glynis, Miss Gwynn, Annie, and Ellen," Mrs. Smithson introduced them.

"Good afternoon," said Maria as she gave Mrs. Smithson the milk can. "I hope you enjoy your visit."

"Would you like some bread and apple butter, Maria? We are having some."

"Yes, ma'am, that would be nice," Maria replied as she found her place at the harvest table.

"Do you work here every day?" Mrs. Glynis asked.

"Oh, no, ma'am. I work on Monday, Wednesday, and Friday afternoons and on Saturdays until lunchtime. I go to school, you know. Mr. McPherson is the teacher and runs the village school," Maria explained. "He's the minister on Sundays at the Presbyterian Church."

"Do you like your classes?" Mrs. Glynis asked. "I'm a teacher, too, in Winchester."

"That's a big school!" Maria exclaimed. "Ours is only a small one, but Mr. McPherson is a good teacher, and we learn a lot."

Mrs. Glynis noticed how pretty she looked, with her big blue eyes and her long blonde hair tied back in a neat bun at the nape of her neck. She wore a simple dress with a shawl over it and rough shoes for working in the dairy. In spite of her small size and her deformity, Maria had a special grace about her and appeared at ease in Mrs. Smithson's company.

"How are you going home today since you stayed later than usual?" asked Mrs. Smithson.

"Oh, Henry McIlwain will drive me in his trap," Maria replied. "I told him to pick me up here at the house. He should be along soon."

Henry was a neighbor, and he often went into the village on Saturday afternoons on business. He would give Maria a lift because Mrs. McPherson insisted the girl be escorted safely home. Sometimes Charlie would take her in his buggy if Henry weren't available. Much to Maria's delight, he had also taught her how to drive the buggy with Madison pulling it.

Charlie and Golden Eagle finally arrived for their tea, and Prince was not far behind them. The old hound dog chose the place of honor beside the open fire. Tired from all of the day's excitement, the dog soon fell asleep and kicked his legs as if he were dreaming of chasing rabbits.

James patted the dog's gray head. "That's all right,

Prince, run and catch them."

"Surely you don't farm this place all by yourself?" Miss Gwynn asked Charlie.

"No, I have Andrew, who comes to help me. We have a lot of neighbors who come to help with the harvest. It's a great time, with everyone working together to get the crops in by the autumn. Then we have Maria here, who helps in the dairy," Charlie replied.

Charlie's farm was well run. He often shod horses belonging to the wagon trains and introduced them to cut iron nails. Sally kept chickens and sold the eggs at the weekly farmers' market in New Town. James attended the Reverend McPherson's school and hoped to continue his studies beyond that.

Charlie accepted a slice of homemade bread and sat down beside the fire for his tea. "It's a great day for visitors," he commented. "Welcome, ladies, I hope you enjoy your stay at Spring Creek Farm. Tomorrow we'll go to Max Stephens' place for the dance. It should be a grand affair. He has hired the best musicians in the valley to play for us. We'll have a great time."

Charlie loved dances. He was already tapping his feet and humming an old tune in anticipation of tomorrow's festivities.

"They say the fiddle is the "devil's box" because it's not mentioned in the Bible like the harp and the dulcimer," observed Mrs. Glynis.

"Don't you believe it!" Charlie laughed. "The musicians in the valley can outplay anyone. They are the best, and they know all the old tunes. I don't think God would object to people having fun, and the devil can stay away. Everyone in the valley was at Max Stephens' dance last September."

"Do you like to dance?" Ellen asked Mrs. Charlie.

"Oh, yes," she replied. "I love the country dancing we do. We have a great caller who guides us through the steps. Is Patrick coming tomorrow to call for us?" she asked her husband.

"I'm not sure," Charlie replied. "Actually, Max himself is getting to be an expert caller. He'll be there, of course, so it should be great fun."

"What kind of instruments do you have?" Miss Gwynn wanted to know.

"We have a bodhrán, a traditional Irish drum, which keeps the beat," Charlie told her. "It's homemade, as are the two fiddles and the banjos. The best musicians are a Negro family who play at most of the dances. They are also great craftsmen. David, Moses, and Seymour play all the traditional tunes and some of their own making. They are renowned throughout the Shenandoah Valley for their music. I am sure Max has got them for this dance because the three brothers are the best. Seymour has a son, Isaac, who is also a good musician. He's only sixteen, but he can play the banjo like you've never heard before."

"What kind of music do you play?" Miss Gwynn asked Charlie.

"I play various traditional tunes. They come from the British Isles and get different words put to them over here. The African slaves have changed the rhythm of the old tunes and added a different beat," Charlie explained. "We mostly dance to Scots-Irish jigs and reels or to square dance tunes."

"You know a lot about music, Charlie," said Mrs. Glynis with admiration, as she helped to clear away the dishes and wash them.

"I got interested when I started to play the fiddle as a boy." Charlie seemed embarrassed.

"Tell me, Charlie, do all redheads have such hidden talents?" asked Annie.

The kitchen filled with laughter as Charlie went to the back wall and took down a homemade fiddle and began to play, "Skip to My Lou."

Fly's in the buttermilk, skip to my Lou
Fly's in the buttermilk, shoo, fly, shoo
Fly's in the buttermilk, skip to my Lou
Skip to my Lou, my darling.

## BREAKFAST

After a comfortable night, James and Charlie were up early. They had to feed the horses and take care of the sheep and milk the cows. Dance or no dance, the chores had to be done.

In the house, Sally rose to feed her hens and to gather the eggs. She moved quickly and quietly, allowing her visitors to sleep in as she made her way to the henhouse to give the chickens their cracked corn.

"What a lovely morning!" she remarked out loud once she was outside. "It's a perfect day for a party."

She let herself into the feed room. "Prince, you stay outside," she told the old dog, who had followed her down from the house. "I can't have you scaring my chickens and reducing their egg production." She measured out the corn in a bucket before letting herself into the chicken house.

The hens gathered around her eagerly as she called to them, "chick, chick, chick," and scattered the cracked corn around their run.

"I brought you bits of apple and some vegetables, too," she said, offering these special treats to one shy and reluctant hen. "Don't allow the other ones to push you out. There you go now. Eat those scraps up."

After all the corn was scattered, Sally refilled the water dishes. Then, taking a basket from the feed room, she filled it with fresh straw and gathered the eggs. There were lovely warm brown ones which their Dominique chickens had laid in the nests Charlie had built. These hens were known for their distinctive black and white feathers.

Although some farmers allowed their hens to run free, the Smithsons' hens had a chicken house with a big run so that the raccoons and opossums could not chase the hens and eat their eggs. They also had a rooster named Tom to warn them of any intruders in the chicken house. That way, Sally had enough eggs for her family and enough to sell at the farmers' market on Saturday mornings in New Town.

Sally gathered two dozen eggs and called Prince, who met her at the chicken house door. Together, they returned home.

Meanwhile, down at the barn, Charlie fed his sheep. They were English Leicester Longwool sheep, and known for their excellent fleece. Charlie turned them out into a big field. James brought in the horses and fed them while Golden Eagle looked after the carriage horses and the pony, Paint.

"What time shall we leave?" he asked Charlie. "How far is it to the Stephens' farm?"

"We'll need to get there about mid-afternoon. Some people will stay the night, but I plan to come home this evening, so we'll take four straps of bells and some lanterns. It'll be dark when we return."

James went into the barn to fetch the bells while his father gave Golden Eagle the lanterns for the carriage.

"Come, now, Golden Eagle, let's go have breakfast. I'm starving."

Accompanied by the Indian coachman, Charlie walked up the hill toward the house. Sally finished the scrambled eggs and was cooking sausage when the men entered the dining kitchen. Charlie went to the springhouse with the milk to cool it right away. He had four Shorthorn cows, a red Scottish breed that was known for its milk and for its good beef quality.

After their tasks were completed, the early risers returned to the house for an inviting breakfast.

"Maria won't be coming this morning, since we are all going to the dance," Charlie explained. "She's planning to go with the McPhersons."

"I hope James gets up enough nerve to ask her to dance. He's been practicing the steps of the Virginia Reel all week. He bows to Prince and then he bows to me as his partner. We went through the spinning wheel dance steps together so he could make sure he knew them." Mrs. Charlie laughed, remembering her own young love, that shy, awkward redhead who later became her husband.

"Come, Golden Eagle, we need to eat some of those fresh eggs. There is also homemade bread with apple butter for breakfast," Charlie offered as his wife served their plates.

"Yes, ma'am, it looks mighty good," Golden Eagle said as he surveyed the well-cooked breakfast and sat down to eat.

Prince looked at Sally with his soulful eyes. He knew better than to beg, but he could look pitiful and she would usually give him a treat. This morning she seemed to have forgotten, so he whined to remind her that he, too, was hungry.

Sally slipped him a piece of sausage under the table so that her husband would not see her giving treats to the dog. Charlie and James had killed and dressed the hogs last fall, and Charlie felt that after all that work, only people should eat the sausage.

A few minutes later, Mrs. Glynis and Miss Gwynn appeared, and, once again, "Mrs. Charlie" offered them a well-prepared meal. Annie and Ellen finally joined them, looking sleepy, but attired in new dresses.

"How nice you look!" Mrs. Glynis told the girls.

"Thank you. Mrs. Taylor helped us make the dresses," Ellen replied. She was delighted that all their hard work had been a success.

"They're lovely," Miss Gwynn agreed. "You'll be the belles of the ball."

"Do you think so?" Ellen asked, blushing from having received two compliments in one morning. Annie acknowledged the compliments with a smile.

"You girls have been busy," remarked Miss Gwynn. "Aren't you the fancy ones in your new dresses?"

They were all eager to get ready and leave early for the dance. Everyone was too dressed up to ride the horses, so they would all go in the two carriages.

These parties were great social affairs in the Shenandoah Valley.

Some of the more prosperous farmers built a ballroom at the back of the second floor of their houses. There, the whole neighborhood would gather for dances. Some people stayed all night and danced until dawn. Charlie, however, preferred to return to his farm. He did not like to leave it unattended.

## BEFORE THE DANCE

Just after lunch, the family left the house in order to arrive on time for the mid-afternoon dance. When they reached the barn, they found that Golden Eagle, not to be outdone by the others, had put red ribbons in the manes of the matched black pair of horses. They had been brushed until they shone, the harness was clean, and the nickel fittings gleamed in the early afternoon sunlight.

"We are all ready to leave," Mrs. Charlie told her husband. "Only Prince looks very sad. He knows everyone is dressed up to go to the dance and he'll be left at home. Even Maria will be with us at the dance. Andrew will be here, though, to look after things—he'll milk the cows and bring them in for the evening. Leave Prince in the barn so he won't follow us."

Charlie and his wife never left the farm unattended. Andrew was a countryman from the mountains of North Carolina. He liked to do odd jobs for people ever since he'd given his eldest son the farm he owned on the other side of New Town. Andrew also played the fiddle, and sometimes Max pressed him into playing at the dances. But today, Andrew had promised to do the chores on Charlie's farm.

"I'm sorry you can't play your fiddle at the dance this year," said Charlie to the older man.

"It's all right," Andrew replied as he leaned over the paddock fence. "It's better that I come and milk your cows and look after your sheep. My fingers are too stiff to play the fiddle."

"I wasn't expecting you to come this early," Charlie said. He backed Jefferson and Madison into their carriage.

"Mr. MacDonald gave me a lift from New Town. I didn't want to wear out my new store-boughten shoes. Hit's a good long ways to here a-walking, you know," Andrew explained. "There's a right smart lot of conveyances on the road. Mr. MacDonald had a passel of young'uns with him, so I rode on one of the horses. He was carrying his family to the dance at Max Stephens' place, yet still a fur piece down the road. Hit's a big spread he's got there, with a ballroom and all," Andrew said, somewhat overwhelmed by Mr. Stephens' affluence.

Later, Charlie explained to his guests that Andrew was from the North Carolina mountains and spoke with a mountain twang. Andrew used old-fashioned words, which were no longer used in less isolated places. Charlie loved to hear him talk, and encouraged his conversation while the guests finished getting ready.

"Andrew, do you know anything about the new idea of keeping the cows at home and not sending them out to the mountain pastures for the summer?"

"A bit," Andrew replied. "You have to build fences, but those who keep stock at home claim they do better because the farmers use the manure on their crops, which makes a bigger yield," Andrew explained as he helped Golden Eagle pull the carriage pole up between the horses and hitch the traces on to the singletrees at the back.

"One of my heifers was injured last summer," Charlie said, picking up the reins of his horses as Andrew hitched them to the carriage. "One of my best heifers is now lame and will remain so. I've decided to keep my cows at home this summer. Andrew, will you help me build some fences?"

"Yes, of course." Andrew laughed. "First, we built fences to keep the cattle out of the chickens' run and the sheep pasture. Now we build the fences to keep the cattle in. But you're right, too many gets injured up in the mountains, and then the strays get stolen and sold to put money in someone else's pocket. Sure, I'll help you build your fences." Andrew laughed again.

Meanwhile, Mrs. Glynis and her sister waited for him to finish tacking up the horses.

"Come ride in my carriage," Charlie told them.

"Ellen, will you come with the ladies and see how you like my horses hitched to a carriage? They may not be as stylish as that black pair of Dr. Mason's, but they can step out too when they like."

Annie, Mrs. Charlie, and James rode out in the carriage with Golden Eagle and the horses. They were now anxious to leave and join the other carriages and wagons on the dirt road to Max Stephens' farm. Andrew stood in the lane and waved them good-bye.

"Do you think Maria will be at the dance?" James asked his mother as they drove down the farm lane. "Do you think if I asked her she'd dance with me?"

Charlie smiled, remembering his own shyness with girls, as he led the team down the road.

"I am sure she would be delighted," Sally replied. "Ask her. After all your practicing with me, you're quite a good dancer."

"Suppose she says no?" James asked anxiously, his voice just above a whisper. "What do I do then?"

"She won't say no," Charlie told him. "She'll be pleased you thought enough of her to want to dance."

"She will?" James wasn't sure. "All right, I'll ask her."

Charlie walked back to the barn to get Mrs. Glynis and Miss Gwynn and drove Jefferson and Madison down the dirt road at a brisk trot. There were several other carriages and wagons traveling to Max Stephens' farm for the dance.

Charlie laughed to himself at James' fear of asking Maria to dance. He would get over his shyness soon enough and would need Charlie's guidance during the next few years. He wondered if Sally remembered his own awkward way with girls when they first met.

## AT THE DANCE

The April afternoon felt warm, and the fruit trees were at the height of their bloom. White blossoms for apples and pink for peaches lined the roadside, interspersed with dogwoods and redbuds, and they made a fairyland of the Shenandoah Valley farms.

Charlie's team soon covered the short distance, and with Golden Eagle's team close behind, they turned into Max Stephens' farm lane.

Max Stephens had a mixed farm, with 350 acres of corn, flax, and wheat. He also raised crossbred Shorthorn cattle. The valley residents were used to sending their cattle up to the mountain meadows to graze in the summer, but injured cattle and the theft of strays made progressive farmers like Max Stephens fence their land and keep their cows at home.

When Charlie and his family and guests arrived at Max's farm, they were surprised to see that the big fields had been fenced and the mixed Shorthorns were grazing peacefully on their home pastures.

Max's home was a typical valley "I" house. It had a two-story front and single-story ell in the back. Upstairs, Max had added a ballroom, where the dances were held.

As they approached the farm, Annie and Mrs. Charlie saw ten other carriages and even more wagons and riding horses.

"There's going to be quite a crowd," James commented. "It'll be a very lively party. I hope some of my school friends will be here."

"You know they will be," his mother replied. "This event is much too important to miss."

"I've never seen so many people!" Annie exclaimed. "It's truly exciting to be here. I've never been to an American dance before."

Max was indeed acquainted with the best musicians

in the valley. Isaac and Joseph each played the fiddle, and Moses played the banjo. They knew all the old tunes: Irish jigs, Virginia reels, and square dances. Isaac's son, Seymour, played the bodhrán, an Irish drum that kept the beat.

The best caller in the valley was Patrick Davidson, and Max had Patrick call at many of his dances. Sometimes, though, Max himself called the reels. He loved to dance and did it with the flair of a real musician. He was also a great clogger. Clogging was a dance that the men performed on a hard floor, always solo or with another man. Women did not dance solo. They danced only with their partners.

When the visitors arrived at Max Stephens' farm, Max's oldest son, Tom, stood at the end of the farm lane to guide the horses and carriages up to the barn.

"Bring the horses around here," he told them. "There's some stabling, and there's a paddock, too."

"Where can Golden Eagle put his horses? They came from Dr. Mason's in Winchester, and I'm responsible for them," Charlie said, as he pulled his team into the farm lane.

"Golden Eagle, follow me. Hello, Mrs. Smithson. I see you've brought company."

"Yes," Sally replied. "We brought Mrs. Glynis and Miss Gwynn, who recently moved to Winchester from Wales."

"Ladies, welcome to Stevens Farm," Max said.

Tom took the reins of the matched pair and led them into the barn. Once there, he helped Sally and Annie climb out of the carriage.

"Golden Eagle, there are two standing stalls at the front of the first level. I'll fork down some hay. The carriage can be stored under the loft." Tom showed them where to go. "Come, ladies, I must speak to Charlie.

Jefferson also needs stabling—he's not to be trusted. James, tell your father to bring his horses in here under the overhang of the first level, or maybe he'd prefer the pasture."

Amid various carriages, wagons, and nervous horses, Sally led Annie, Ellen, Mrs. Glynis, and Miss Gwynn out of the barn and into the side yard. Stepping gingerly and following Tom, they finally reached the front door of the house.

"I'll tell Charlie you're at the house," Tom promised. Then he rushed off toward the barn to direct the horses and wagons that pulled into the farm lane.

Sally was welcomed at the front door by Max Stephens' wife, Helen.

"Oh, Sally, what a treat to see you!" Mrs. Stephens exclaimed. "I'm so glad you came and brought your Welsh friends. Do come in and have some refreshment after your drive."

Just then, Max Stephens entered the hall. "The dancing should start soon—I understand the musicians have arrived," he informed his guests, who were now gathered in the sitting room. "Our son, Tad, is taking Moses and Seymour up to the ballroom. Isaac and Joseph are carrying in the instruments, so the music will start at any time now."

Max Stephens guided his guests away from the refreshment table and up to the ballroom. Annie and Ellen followed, anxious to hear the musicians. Chairs stood against the walls, and the girls found two together in which to sit. They eagerly scanned the room after smiling at two ladies sitting near them.

"Have you heard of this new dance in Vienna?" Mrs. Yoder asked her neighbor, Mrs. Schmidt, as they watched the dancers gather for the Virginia Reel.

Max planned to call the first set and encouraged Ellen and Annie to join the dance, each of them partnered by one of Max's sons. The musicians played "Turkey in the Straw," an old favorite for country dancing. Max stood in front of the musicians, his feet tapping the floor to the rhythm of the music.

"All right, ladies and gents, it's time to begin with the Virginia Reel. Let's have the men in a line on the left side and the ladies on the right side. That's good, hurry along and listen to my patter:

>Now don't be bashful, don't be shy,
>Step on out and give it a try.
>We'll walk you through and show you the way,
>With Isaac, Moses, Joseph, and me.
>So you can learn; the steps are easy,
>'Cause it's our plan to have fun today.
>Isaac and Jospeh have their fiddles.
>Come on, Moses, it's time to play.
>
>It's called 'Turkey in the Straw,'
>The finest music you've ever heard,
>Now, that turkey is a rare old bird.
>Dance to the tune, and you'll have fun,
>Come on and join us, everyone."
>You men turn and face your girl
>Is everyone ready? Now give her a whirl.
>
>Go back to your place
>To hear me sing.
>Now forward again, with a zing
>Now give your lady
>A two-handed swing.
>Then back to your place while I sing
>Let's make the very rafters ring.

Charlie smiled as he and Sally started to dance. He swung her around and raised his arms to make an arch for the dancers to go under as they returned to their positions.

Ellen found herself paired with Ben, one of Max's sons, and they tried to dance the Virginia Reel. To her surprise, Ellen found the steps unfamiliar. Suddenly, she got her feet tangled up and nearly fell.

"Oh, dear." She blushed. "I'm all out of tune today."

"Never mind," said Ben as he showed Ellen the steps, and they tried them again. "Relax," Ben told her. "I'll show you how it goes." This time, Ellen found she could dance the Virginia Reel after all.

Ellen laughed as they gracefully followed the lively music. "It's not like dancing in Wales," she remarked as she copied Ben's lead and do-si-doed with the rest of the dancers. Max Stephens called the steps in sing-song rhythm, which helped her to follow them.

Annie fared less well with Tom Stephens, another one of Max's sons. Tom put his whole heart into the dance, but, unfortunately, he lacked the grace and a sense of rhythm. Annie felt like a sack of beans from the fields as Tom swung her around in a clumsy manner. Finally, he broke loose from Annie and clogged on the hard wooden floor with a lot of stomping, but with no sense of the music rhythm.

Tom continued clogging and hardly noticed Annie. When Charlie saw that her partner had abandoned her, he excused himself from his wife and asked Annie to dance with him. Then he guided her away from Tom and his stomping.

"Who's the pretty girl that's dancing with Charlie?" Mrs. Yoder asked.

"That's Annie Jones, a member of the Welsh family Charlie drove down from Philadelphia last summer," Mrs. Schmidt replied.

"Look at that dark hair and those blue eyes. Charlie knows how to pick out the best-looking girls to partner at the dances," Mrs. Yoder observed.

"Really," Mrs. Schmidt said, looking shocked. "He's rescuing her from Tom Stephens. Charlie's a perfect gentleman."

"Yes," agreed Mrs. Yoder. "But he also enjoys dancing with a pretty young girl."

Mrs. Yoder had lived in the Shenandoah Valley for a long time. She attended all the dances, but she only danced with Herr Yoder, her husband of thirty years. Mrs. Yoder liked coming to Max Stephens' socials and was usually at his house a good half hour before the party started and was the last to leave in the evening. Max put up with her because he liked Hans Yoder, who was very knowledgeable about farm animals and had introduced him to the new idea of spreading manure on the crops to produce a larger yield.

Mrs. Stephens also tolerated the opinionated German ladies to please her husband. Although Mrs. Yoder could be difficult, she always brought three freshly baked loaves of bread and several jars of homemade peach jam as her contribution to the refreshments.

"Sometimes the Germans can be very generous," Helen told Sally when they met at the refreshment table. Helen usually left the dance floor early so that she could finish preparing the food and drinks before the dancers came downstairs. Sally accompanied her to help with the preparations.

"Mrs. Schmidt always brings homemade wine. They have a small winery with very-high-quality grapes. The wine they make is like the wines of the Mosel, the German part of the French Moselle near Koblenz. The German ladies always help with the cleaning up after the dance," Helen said as she poured a glass of wine and offered it to Sally. "This is a German wine from one of the farms in the Shenandoah Valley. It's very light and refreshing."

When the music changed, Tom looked up and saw that Annie was dancing with Charlie. He asked another girl to dance the next reel with him. Meanwhile, Max Stephens asked Sally to dance.

Max loved to dance and was especially light on his feet. He grew up in the Tidewater region of Virginia and moved to Richmond as a young man. He left soon afterward and went west to the Shenandoah Valley, where he fell in love with the beautiful countryside and decided to settle there. Life in Richmond, the capital city of Virginia, felt too cramped both socially and physically. Max sought freedom from Richmond's social restrictions and its conservative way of life. After meeting Helen in Richmond, the two decided to live in the Shenandoah Valley, where they could feel free. Max's father was disappointed, but his eldest son, Edmond, was well suited for the life of a politician. Edmond joined the Virginia Assembly and became a friend of Jefferson's.

The music was fast, but the couples danced with the beat and enjoyed themselves. The musicians finally brought the dance to a close, and Max, his face red from exertion, decided it was time to stop and go down to the dining room for refreshments. The musicians put down their fiddles and banjo and followed Max with his sons and the dancers. The ballroom soon became empty, except for two women busy with their own conversation.

Mrs. Yoder and Mrs. Schmidt remained in their chairs lined against the ballroom wall. Now that the music was over, they could chat more easily.

"You were saying something about this new French dance called the waltz," Mrs. Schmidt reminded her neighbor. "I've heard it is quite risqué, with the man's arm around the lady's waist!"

Mrs. Schmidt liked to show off her smattering of French. She had once lived on the Moselle River near the French border and fancied that she could speak the language.

"It's not a French dance. It's from Austria. Can you imagine a man taking such liberties with a lady not his wife?" Mrs. Yoder looked surprised at such impropriety. She took out her fan to blow away the sinful influences of such behavior. "I heard the French have disapproved of the waltz, so it must be very risqué. Who knows what will come out of Austria with its Turkish influences!"

"Oh, the Turks only introduced coffee into Vienna when they fled the Vienna Woods around 1680 and left all of their coffee pots behind. There were no risqué dances," Mrs. Schmidt assured her.

"I heard the English approved of this waltz dance, but not the Germans," Mrs. Yoder continued. "We Germans have better morals than either the French or the English. We would never approve of such inappropriate dances. It really must be quite disgraceful because, with the French still trying to recover after the war, you would think they would not have time to worry about dances."

"Yes, it's quite extraordinary," Mrs. Schmidt agreed.

"What's the name of that fellow who stopped Napoleon in Belgium at Waterloo?" Mrs. Yoder wondered.

"You mean the Duke of Wellington? His full name is Arthur Wellesley, and he's from Trim, the same town where my neighbor lives, north of Dublin. The Irish are great warriors, you know. They and the Highland Scots in all those fancy tartan kilts are wonderful fighters. What a sight it is to see those highland regiments in all their rigout on parade with their bagpipes and drums."

"Yes, the Duke of Wellington. I didn't realize he came from Ireland. I guess it would take an Irishman to defeat Napoleon. Every other country had tried and failed except the Russians. But it was really the Russian winter that defeated the Grande Armée and drove it out of Moscow," Mrs. Yoder confided.

"The Duke of Wellington with the British Forces finally defeated the Grande Armée and Napoleon at Waterloo in 1815," Mrs. Schmidt added. Together, the two women left the ballroom to go down to the dining room for refreshments.

They found the table laden with good things to eat. Helen Stephens welcomed them and offered them punch, little cakes, and tea sandwiches.

"I admit the French make good wines," said Mrs. Yoder. She saw that Mrs. Stephens and Mrs. Smithson were discussing wine and inserted herself into their conversation. "It's their morals I'm concerned about. Our Mr. Jefferson became enamored with French culture, and I'm afraid he took on some of their ideas. I think he found the Germans too moral for his tastes."

"At his death four years ago, Mr. Jefferson left a wonderful legacy—a university to teach the young men of Virginia how to become leaders in this state. He was a good man and could see into Virginia's future," argued Sally.

"I don't know about his morals," replied Mrs. Yoder. "But with the French influence and his being a redhead, Mr. Jefferson needed watching." She returned to the refreshment table.

"Are your Welsh friends enjoying themselves? They seem a lively group of visitors," Helen asked as she poured Sally some more wine.

"Oh, yes," Sally replied. "The young folks are dancing like veterans. My son, James, and Maria danced every set. He was scared about coming, but he's certainly enjoying himself. He learned the steps in my kitchen, and we danced until my feet hurt."

Helen laughed. Mrs. Glynis and Miss Gwynn approached to make conversation with their hostess.

"How do you like America?" Mrs. Stephens asked the two Welsh ladies.

"It's very different from Wales," Mrs. Glynis

explained. "We're still settling in. So far, we've found it to be a beautiful country full of the most generous and interesting people. Have you always lived in the Shenandoah Valley?"

"No, I grew up in Charles City County, Virginia" Mrs. Stephens replied. "My father had three boys to educate, and I was left to do as I liked. It was a busy time on our farm, and I needed space to grow up. I met Max when I was eighteen, and then I didn't see him again until three years later when he came to Richmond to visit his uncle, John Stephens. By then, my family thought I'd never marry, because I wanted to become a teacher."

Max greeted Charlie with a handshake. "We have a great crowd this afternoon," he said, his face flush from the exertion of calling the dances. "Everyone from this part of the valley is here, and more will come this evening when their farm chores will allow them to leave home."

Charlie nodded. "I brought some newcomers— several Welsh ladies who have recently settled in Winchester. They were anxious to see how valley folk entertain themselves. They're talking with your wife and enjoying your hospitality."

James was hot and breathless from trying to keep the dance steps straight and not fall over Maria's new shoes. "Come on, let's get something cool to drink."

The guests filled the dining room with talk and laughter. James led her upstairs once more to offer Maria a cold drink. Here it was less noisy, and they could sit down and chat together.

"I never thought I could dance without tramping on your feet," James said with a shy grin. "I've only ever danced with mother in our kitchen."

"It was fun," Maria said, her eyes sparkling with happiness and pride. "We didn't miss a step."

"I like the tune 'Turkey in the Straw'," James replied. "It's got a good beat."

"Our arch was well done. At least no one's hair got caught in my fingers." Maria giggled at the thought. "Sometimes the ladies don't bend down far enough, but today's arch was perfect."

After they finished their refreshments, the guests returned to the ballroom for more dancing. Max reappeared, and Isaac and Seymour got ready to play their fiddles. Moses tuned his banjo, and Joseph picked up the spoons to drum on the wooden edge of the bodhrán. Then the couples took their places for a second Virginia Reel.

The line formed almost immediately, and, once again, James led Maria out onto the floor. He saw his father and mother join the line. Charlie loved to dance, and he and Sally always made an attractive couple.

Ellen was again paired with Ben. Tad asked Annie to dance, and she hoped he would be a more accomplished partner than Tom. Mrs. Glynis and Miss Gwynn also found partners with two of Charlie's neighbors. The music began with the bodhrán, two fiddles, and the banjo. The rest of the company clapped in time.

As evening approached, most of the dancers stopped for supper. Some had brought food to share with their neighbors, while some of the farmers felt the need to return home to take care of their animals.

Reverend McPherson came into the room in search of Maria.

"We must get home," he told her. "Your mother is anxious about her chickens. Apparently, she saw a fox this morning sniffing around the chicken house, and she wants to make sure her hens are not in danger."

"What fun we've had!" Maria told her father. Her eyes were bright with excitement and pleasure. "James knew all the steps, and he taught them to me."

"Good! Come along now. The family is waiting at the front door. The spring wagon is ready to leave."

Maria and James walked together to the front door,

where they found Maria's brothers and sisters waiting.

"Let me help you up," James offered his arm in support as she put her foot on the narrow wooden step.

"What fun!" exclaimed Maria, for the second time. "I'm breathless from the dancing. Good-bye, James!" She sat down as the horses walked forward, and waved until James was lost from sight amid the numerous wagons leaving Max Stephens' farm.

"Come on, James," said Charlie, as he put a hand on his son's shoulder and led him down the hill. "It's time for us to get on home. Andrew will be awaiting our return. Golden Eagle has gone ahead with his horses. Your mother will find Mrs. Glynis and Miss Gwynn and the girls."

"What a lot of horses! There are wagons and carriages of all descriptions," said James, as he and his father entered the barn.

"Yes, it's been a wonderful neighborhood gathering," Golden Eagle remarked. He and John, another one of Max's sons, led Madison and Jefferson out of the barnyard.

"Let me help," said Charlie, as he took his horses away from the congestion of carriages and wagons parked nearby.

The horses were soon put to the carriage, and Charlie took the reins and drove them back to Max's house to pick up his wife and their guests.

"Golden Eagle, may I ride home with you?" James asked, as he helped the coachman with the horses.

"Yes, of course," said the older man. "Did you have a good time, James? I saw you dancing with Maria. You looked like an expert."

"I had a great time," replied James. "I never thought I could dance so well and knew so many different steps."

## PINE BLOSSOM

Some weeks after the dance, Robert looked up at the road on the ridge above the barn. He saw Madison, carrying Charlie and Spotted Deer, go around a bend and disappear from sight.

"Where's Spotted Deer going?" Robert asked Old Cyrus. "And why is Charlie with him?"

"Charlie's come to take Spotted Deer to visit his sweetheart," Old Cyrus informed him. "He's coming back tomorrow."

"Sweetheart? Is Spotted Deer in love?" Robert asked, surprised by the revelation.

"Yes," replied Cyrus. "She lives in Strasburg, twenty miles up the valley from here. Her name is Pine Blossom."

"Pine Blossom? What kind of name is that?"

"It's an Indian name, of course," Old Cyrus replied. "She's Shawnee like Spotted Deer, and a beautiful young girl. She's been in love with him for quite a while now."

"I didn't realize Spotted Deer had a sweetheart," Robert said, incredulous about the lad's romance. Robert got out his fishing gear and went below the barn to dig a few earthworms for bait.

Meanwhile, as Charlie rode Madison with Spotted Deer toward Winchester, he gently asked the young man what he planned to do when they reached Strasburg.

"I want to marry Pine Blossom," Spotted Deer told him. "But I'm not sure when it will happen. I'm anxious to get settled, but I feel I can't leave Robert. He's been so unhappy since his wife's death. I don't know what to do."

Charlie felt touched by the lad's loyalty. "Maybe Robert will remarry," he suggested. "He's so mixed up in his own sadness he's forgotten about Mrs. Glynis. She's a lovely woman from his own country, and they have a lot in common."

"But he'll never get remarried the way things are going. All he can do is fish," replied Spotted Deer. "He's crazy about it. The trout have gotten wise to him now and avoid his bait. We need to get Robert interested in something else."

Madison brought Charlie and Spotted Deer out onto Valley Road, and they left the mountains and woods behind. The Shenandoah Valley and the town of Winchester lay before them. Charlie stopped briefly in Will's Tavern.

"Good to see you, Charlie," Will told him as they rode into the stable yard to rest and to water Madison. Will joined them at the tavern for a quick meal. Afterward, Charlie and Spotted Deer remounted their big horse and continued to Strasburg. They still had about eighteen miles to cover.

Pine Blossom lived with a German family just outside of the village. Unlike Winchester, which was settled by the English and by the Scots-Irish, German Palatines settled Strasburg. The Stuart Queen Anne of England, who died in 1714, helped these Protestants come to the colonies. During the War of Independence, out of loyalty to her, many German Palatines found themselves on the wrong side of the war. Many left the Valley for Canada, but the town of Strasburg still maintained a healthy German population.

Pine Blossom, like Maria and Spotted Deer, was an orphan. She was gravely ill when the local German doctor, Andreas Becker, found the tiny child, only about two years old, left in the waiting room of his office one cold December afternoon. The little girl would have died but for the careful nursing of his wife, Freda, who warmed her by the fire and gave her some hot soup.

"Do you have a name, little one?" Freda Becker asked the child.

"I Pine Blossom," the little one told her in English.

After she drank the hot soup, the little girl fell asleep in the good woman's arms.

Two months of diligent inquiry as to the child's identity brought no success. Freda Becker decided to keep her and raise her as her own. Pine Blossom became a lovely, healthy child, and then an accomplished young woman.

Frau Becker had four other children, but this little girl touched her deeply, and soon Pine Blossom was a fully accepted member of the family. Dr. Becker loved her as his own daughter, but he also felt strongly that she should keep her Indian name. He hoped that someday, she would come to understand her heritage and be able to share her earliest memories with someone who might also understand them. For this reason, he was very curious when he learned that another Indian child, Spotted Deer, was being raised by Dr. Hughes and his wife in Winchester.

Dr. Becker invited Spotted Deer to Strasburg to meet Pine Blossom when both children were still very young. They became fast friends, and although they didn't see each other very often, they grew fond of each other over the years. Now this friendship had grown into romantic love.

When Spotted Deer decided he wanted to marry Pine Blossom, he first consulted Old Cyrus about the matter.

"Go ask her, lad," Cyrus encouraged him. "She'll be a jewel like my Rachel. Go down to Strasburg and talk to her."

"How would it work?" Spotted Deer asked. "Where would she live?"

"I've decided to play Cupid," Old Cyrus informed the young man. "I saw in Will's Tavern a man who built himself a cabin, but he's moving elsewhere and he wants someone to occupy it so the place isn't bothered by vandals."

"How do you know about Cupid?" Spotted Deer asked. "Isn't he a Greek god of some kind?"

"I had a friend in North Carolina named Cupid Maxwell whose father could read books until his eyes gave out. He told me Cupid was the god of love who pricked people with his arrows to make them fall in love with each other. I wish I could prick Robert like that. There is Mrs. Glynis, as nice a lady as ever you'd meet. Yet he can't see her for fishing. He's blinded by trout and earthworms. What's wrong with him?"

Old Cyrus tapped his unlit pipe against the pasture gate in disgust. "He can see those rambunctious sheep, and he can see the fish. I wish my Rachel were here to talk some sense into that man." Cyrus nearly tripped over Danny, who lay at his feet, as he continued to fill his pipe.

Spotted Deer opened the gate and led the calf, Rambeau, out into the paddock, and then returned to milk the cows. Cyrus caught the lad by the arm as he went to the barn with the milk cans.

"Spotted Deer, go down to Strasburg and ask Pine Blossom to marry you," Cyrus advised. "You love her, and that's all that matters. I'll get in touch with Will Holliday and make some necessary arrangements."

That conversation had occurred two weeks earlier, and now Spotted Deer was riding with Charlie to Strasburg to offer Pine Blossom his hand.

Frau Becker had received a note from Charlie, which Will Holliday sent down with the driver of the stagecoach. The good German housewife told Pine Blossom that Charlie and Spotted Deer planned to arrive on the following Saturday for a visit. The note indicated that this might be a visit of some importance, so she instructed Pine Blossom to wear her Sunday dress. Then Frau Becker consulted with an Indian woman, whom she knew from the market, about Shawnee customs.

"I have some beads and some special ceremonial

jewelry that the girls wear. Just have Pine Blossom dress in her usual church clothes, and I'll add something I think is appropriate for the occasion."

Pine Blossom had grown into a slender, pretty, twenty-year-old girl. The Beckers raised her as a Christian. She spoke German in the family and spoke English with a German accent everywhere else. Her brown eyes, her braided long straight hair, and her dark complexion made it clear to most valley people that she was at least part Indian. She also had gracious manners and a winning smile.

Frau Becker saw to it that Pine Blossom attended the Strasburg school, which was run by the Lutheran minister. As a young girl, she caught on well and could soon read and write. She often helped her brothers and sisters with their schoolwork. Frau Becker had hoped that Pine Blossom would one day find an Indian lad to marry. A few Indian families still lived in the Shenandoah Valley, but most of the Shawnees had moved west toward the Ohio River.

Pine Blossom's brothers were very protective of their little sister, so Frau Becker knew that whoever asked for Pine Blossom's hand had to be very special. She had known Spotted Deer from a young age and decided that he was a good lad and an honest worker. She told her husband, Andreas, that she thought they would do well together.

"Yes, that's a good match," he agreed. "But I shall miss Pine Blossom's cheerful voice and her ready smile. She will always be a true daughter of mine."

Andreas Becker's grandfather had come to the American colonies as a mercenary soldier during the War of Independence. He was badly wounded and remained in the colonies. As a young man, he had settled in Lancaster County in Pennsylvania and worked on a farm that belonged to a family from the Rhineland's Palatinate region. When his wounds healed, he struck out on his own and came down to Strasburg in the Shenandoah Valley.

Here, he had worked odd jobs on other German farms until he'd saved enough money to buy a few acres for himself.

Andreas remembered his grandfather, who spoke little English. He became his grandfather's interpreter. The old soldier had died when the boy was twelve.

Andreas's father, Rolf, added a few more acres to the original farm, and now Andreas had inherited them. His father built a barn and enlarged the German-style house. Here he had brought his wife Freda to live after his father died. As a young man, Andreas studied medicine and became a doctor.

"Where will Pine Blossom get married?" the doctor asked his wife.

"In the Lutheran church, of course, like a proper German Christian," Freda replied. She was unbending about her German-speaking church.

"Does the lad speak German?" Andreas inquired. "He may not understand the marriage ceremony. Get the Reverend McPherson to come as well to do the vows in English, just to be sure."

Freda sniffed, but said she would remember to ask the Scotsman to come. Meanwhile, she tidied her already pristine clean house and told Pine Blossom to dress in her church clothes, as they expected company.

## SPOTTED DEER'S COURTSHIP

When Spotted Deer and Charlie reached Strasburg, the lad became so nervous about his quest that he could hardly stand up when he slid off Madison's broad back.

"I can't do it!" Spotted Deer insisted. "It seemed easy enough in Winchester, but I'm terrified here."

"Go on," Charlie encouraged him. "Just go up to the front door and knock."

"Suppose she refuses me?"

Spotted Deer steadied himself and did as Charlie bade. To her suitor's great relief, Pine Blossom answered the door.

"Yes?" she inquired from within. "Who is it?"

He swallowed hard. "Spotted Deer. I've ridden down from Winchester with Charlie Smithson, and I wish to ask you something," the Indian lad replied. "May I come in?"

Pine Blossom recognized Spotted Deer's voice. "Yes, of course," she said and opened the door.

Charlie watched the performance and shook his head. "He'll never ask her," he said to himself. "Spotted Deer's scared speechless."

The lad, once inside the neat German house, stood in the parlor and just stared at Pine Blossom.

"Come sit down." She welcomed her frightened suitor. "You look terribly ill."

"I came to ask you something." His voice squeaked. "I want you to marry me. Will you, Pine Blossom? I love you."

The girl did not reply, but ran into the kitchen for a wet towel to put on the young man's forehead. "I think he's about to faint," she whispered to her adoptive mother "He's come to ask me to marry him, and the shock of it has him paralyzed with fright."

The two of them quickly got some cold spring water

to cool Spotted Deer's brow, and Mrs. Becker found some cold coffee, which she reheated. When Pine Blossom reentered the parlor, her suitor lay on the sofa almost in a faint.

"Here, drink this, and put the cold cloth on your forehead," Pine Blossom instructed. "You'll be all right again."

Spotted Deer sat up and drank the sugared, reheated coffee.

"I came to see you and to bring you this beaded necklace. It's all I have from my mother, who died shortly after I was born. My parents were both Shawnee. Dr. Hughes took care of me after my father left for the Ohio Valley. The doctor and his wife, Miss Jane, raised me. I was apprenticed to Old Cyrus at fourteen, so then he became my mentor," Spotted Deer explained.

"I know about your heritage. I have one like it because I was found by the Beckers. They took me in and raised me," Pine Blossom explained. "But you know that."

Spotted Deer handed Pine Blossom the colorful beaded work that his mother had left him. "Will you accept this necklace as a symbol of the sincerity of my troth?"

Pine Blossom nodded and put the string of Indian beads over her head. "I accept," she replied, and gave him her hand.

"Please don't tell Charlie Smithson I acted such a fool," Spotted Deer begged her. "He'd laugh at my courtship, and I couldn't stand that."

They sat together in the parlor, and Mrs. Becker discreetly remained in the kitchen. She had hoped the two young Indians would like each other, but she never told her private thoughts to anyone other than her husband. She felt it might cause bad luck if she voiced her wishes for them.

When Charlie returned later that evening with his new fleet-footed pony hitched to a cart, both Pine Blossom and Spotted Deer were smiling. Then Charlie knew that the suit had gone well and that they would soon celebrate a wedding.

Dr. Becker offered Charlie some cold locust pod beer, and, together with Mrs. Becker, they toasted the young couple's happiness. "I hope you will be very happy together. He raised his stein.

"May all of your troubles be little ones," Charlie told them, winking at Spotted Deer.

After the celebration, Charlie took Spotted Deer back to New Town to stay the night with him. The lad seemed exhausted from his day's adventures.

Dr. and Mrs. Becker, with Pine Blossom at their side, waved the travelers good-bye. Charlie drove the pony and cart away from the neat German farm and headed north to New Town.

"Don't you dare tell Old Cyrus I acted such a fool," Spotted Deer warned Charlie as they drove along. "It just overwhelmed me. I have never asked a girl to marry me before."

"That's our secret." Charlie laughed, remembering his own courtship. "I hope you're able to stand upright on your wedding day."

"I do, too," Spotted Deer agreed. "It's rather important, you know, for me to keep my wits and say all the correct words. Will I have to say them in German *and* in English, do you suppose?"

"It doesn't matter. Just so you live by them. And create a happy home. That's what's important," Charlie reminded him, as the pony trotted toward New Town. The white blossoms of the apple trees lent their fragrance to the soft spring evening.

Spotted Deer smiled at his bold act of courtship. "I don't know how I ever got the courage to ask her," he whispered aloud.

## SPOTTED DEER'S WEDDING

The date for the wedding was set for after the planting and lambing seasons were finished. "May's a good time," Charlie told Spotted Deer. "Get married in May."

Mrs. Yoder and Mrs. Schmidt came to visit Mrs. Becker to help her make a simple white dress for Pine Blossom.

"The lambs are born, the gardens are planted, and crops are seeded," said Mrs. Yoder. "It's getting warm. May is a perfect time for a wedding."

Pine Blossom had little to say about the date. The older women, who knew all about marriage, had decided on May.

"That will also give us enough time to make your dress," Mrs. Yoder explained. "We can't fashion a wedding dress within a few days. It takes time, my dear, to make it beautiful and in the latest fashion."

Pine Blossom soon realized that the German ladies had quickly taken over her wedding plans. So, she put on her bonnet and walked to Mr. Thomas' general store. She decided to get out of the ladies' company and to ask Mrs. Thomas, the wife of the storeowner, for the special kind of sewing thread she needed for her dress. The German ladies could stay at home and work without her suggestions, which they simply ignored.

Meanwhile, Charlie decided to go to Winchester to see Robert and to check on Spotted Deer. "I'd better go and make sure Spotted Deer hasn't died of fright," Charlie told Sally. "If he's as scared as he was when he proposed to Pine Blossom, I can't imagine how he's feeling now."

"I've made Spotted Deer a good shirt, and Mrs. Yoder has just finished another. He'll also need a dark suit," Mrs. Charlie said. "I found a good one that Mr. Blake had in his general store. He said the tailor made it for Frederick Wilson, and it didn't fit right. So I swapped four pounds of country butter for the abandoned suit. Mr. Blake was delighted with the butter."

"You're quite the trader," Charlie teased his wife as he drank a final cup of tea and prepared for the drive to Winchester in order to deliver the suit and the shirts. "I'll take the new pony and trap," he said. Charlie had gotten the pony recently from Max, who had found it injured and left on his farm, tied to a post near the barn. He never found who owned the little trotter, and after Max got the horse sound, he swap him to Charlie.

"That poor pony needs a name," Sally remarked. "You've had him a month now and still the little fellow has no name. Why don't you call him Pirate?"

"That's a grand name. I'll use it," Charlie said, as he left the house. "Here comes Maria. I'll say a quick hello, but I need to be leaving now for Winchester."

Charlie greeted Maria as he met her and Reverend McPherson in the farm lane.

"Good morning, Charlie," Reverend McPherson greeted him. "I brought Maria myself today. I'll pick her up later."

"Sally's inside," Charlie said. "I'm off to Winchester to deliver a wedding garment to Spotted Deer."

"Good morning, Mr. Charlie," Maria waved. "I'd hoped you would take that new pony. He's really a trotter. I'll go in and tell Mrs. Charlie I'm here."

Charlie met James at the barn. James had Pirate already hooked to the cart.

"Andrew's coming today, so you can come with me," Charlie told his son. "I'm delivering a wedding suit for Spotted Deer and will return this evening."

James ran to the house to tell Sally he would accompany his father to Winchester and waved good-bye to Reverend McPherson.

"We won't stay long," James promised his mother.

"That will be a first time," Sally replied. "If I know

Charlie, he'll need a long time to check up on his friends at Will's Tavern."

Charlie wrapped the new wedding clothes in two torn pieces of fabric and secured them in an oak basket. Then he placed the package in the cart, and he and James climbed in, waved good-bye to Sally and Maria, and guided Pirate toward Winchester. The little fellow leaped forward and trotted like a racehorse down the dirt road.

Over an hour and a half later, James and Charlie turned off the road and rode along the ridge above Robert's farm.

"What brings you here?" Old Cyrus asked, happy to see them. "There are no stock sales today."

"We've come with a gift for Spotted Deer. Is he here?" Charlie asked as he and James brought Pirate down from the ridge at a walk.

"He and Robert went fishing," Old Cyrus replied. "I'm the only one who gets any work done around this farm. Danny and I are worn out with sheep and cows."

Cyrus took the little trotter's bridle and led him into the barn

"We have brought Spotted Deer his wedding clothes," Charlie said. "Sally sent him two shirts, and she found him a suit in New Town."

"Oh," replied Cyrus "I'm grateful to you because Spotted Deer is worrying Robert and me to death about his wedding. We certainly thank you for solving that problem. Now solve the one about this broken harness."

Charlie unhitched Pirate and put him in an empty stall and forked in some hay. Old Cyrus whistled across the valley. An answering whistle came from farther downstream. A few minutes later, breathless from chasing the ewes out of the woods, Spotted Deer appeared.

"Hello, Charlie, James," Spotted Deer welcomed his visitors. "What brings you here today?"

"Your wedding," Charlie said with a laugh. "We

have brought your wedding garments."

"My wedding garments," Spotted Deer repeated, not able to believe what he heard.

"Sally found a suit that will fit you," Charlie explained, handing Spotted Deer the carefully wrapped package of clothes.

Spotted Deer smiled as he undid the bundle of wedding garments. "Oh, Charlie," he gasped, overcome by his friend's generosity. "These are lovely shirts, and the suit is beautiful. I've never seen anything so elegant."

"Spotted Deer, try on the jacket," James urged him.

"Oh, no, it's too good. I'll have to wash and get Cyrus to cut my hair before I try on these special clothes."

Later, after a swim in the steam, Spotted Deer tried on one of the shirts and the suit.

"It's truly beautiful, Charlie," he said. "Feel the jacket—it's soft." The Indian lad felt amazed to receive such a marvelous gift.

"Mama made one of the shirts. Mrs. Yoder made the other. Do they fit you well enough?" James asked.

"They are wonderful, and I am forever grateful to Mrs. Charlie for her kindness, and to Mrs. Yoder as well," Spotted Deer said, choking on his tears of appreciation

"Where is Robert?" Charlie asked, realizing he had not seen him since that morning. "Fishing again?"

"No, he's gone to see Yorweth about getting the services of a bull for our cows," Old Cyrus replied. "He's gotten interested in visiting the Welshman. He takes Light Horse Harry and goes off for the better part of the day."

"It's more useful than fishing," Spotted Deer remarked. "I'm sick of fishing. His interest in the Welsh couple will give the earthworms a chance to recover."

"Yes, we're getting mighty low on bait," Old Cyrus added.

"Where will your wedding be held?" Charlie asked the lad.

"In the Lutheran church in Strasburg, at eleven o'clock in the morning, two weeks from Saturday," Spotted Deer told him. "Mr. Holliday wants me to come into Winchester and spend the night on the Friday before so I can get my hair cut by a good barber. He'll give me the overnight stay and the haircut as a wedding present. He also found us a little house in town, so Pine Blossom won't be isolated in the country," Spotted Deer replied, excited to imagine his new life.

Spotted Deer asked Old Cyrus to be his best man, because he regarded it as a mark of respect. But Old Cyrus felt uncomfortable in church, and he did not wish to stand in front of a congregation he did not know. He happened to look down at his fingers, and he thought he would never get them clean enough to be in a wedding.

"My fingernails are too dirty to be the best man," Old Cyrus explained. "I'll never get them clean in time. Ask Robert. With two daughters, it might do him good to get some practice with weddings."

"Yes," Spotted Deer replied, feeling hurt because his mentor had rejected his compliment. "I'll ask Robert."

Old Cyrus fussed about his clothes and got Spotted Deer to cut his hair. Then, as the time drew near, Cyrus began to wear gloves to do his work.

"I need you to cut my fingernails and get the dirt from under them," he told Robert the week before the wedding. "My hands look cleaner since I'm wearing these gloves Charlie gave me."

Will Holliday, upon hearing about Old Cyrus' sudden concern about his appearance, asked Charlie to come up from New Town and call in at the next stock sale.

"I hear this forthcoming wedding has got Old Cyrus in a great fuss about what he's to wear," Will told Charlie when the two men met. "I have an old suit of clothes of my brother-in-law's. He hardly wore it, and Alexander Davis, the local tailor, has brushed it and put in a few stitches. See if Cyrus would like it. Tell him also to come into Winchester to try the suit on and to have Matt Wilson cut his hair. We'll get Cyrus fancied up for this wedding."

"He's refused to be the best man," Charlie told Will. "But he'll have to go in honor of Spotted Deer."

"We will get him ready and dressed up enough to go into any church, never mind a German Lutheran one." Will laughed as he led Charlie into the bar. "You wait. Old Cyrus will outshine us all."

Later that week, Charlie arrived at Robert's farm driving Pirate. "It's all arranged," he told Old Cyrus. "You're to come into Winchester with me for a store bought haircut and a fitting for a suit Will Holliday has got for you to wear at Spotted Deer's wedding."

Old Cyrus couldn't believe what Charlie told him. "I'm not the best man. Robert has that job, so I don't need to be too handsome. My fingernails are clean at last." Old Cyrus pulled off his gloves to show Charlie his hands.

"Come along, Old Cyrus, we are off to town to see about your clothes for the wedding." Charlie helped him into the cart. Then, after a word with Spotted Deer about how long they would be away, Charlie turned Pirate and regained the ridge road.

Spotted Deer went to tell Robert of Old Cyrus' absence and not to expect his return until that evening.

Once in Winchester, Will Holliday had Matt cut Cyrus' hair and fingernails and asked the tailor to fit the hand-me-down suit.

"I look like an aristo-crate," Cyrus said proudly as he looked at himself in the mirror in Davis' tailor shop. "I am almost handsome."

"Yes, you are," agreed Charlie. "Now go to the wedding in Strasburg with your head held high."

"I surely shall," Cyrus said, and the two men entered Will's Tavern.

On a beautiful May morning, the friends of Spotted

Deer and Pine Blossom made their way toward Strasburg.

Golden Eagle brought Mrs. Glynis, Miss Gwynn, Ellen, and Annie in Dr. Mason's carriage down to Strasburg for the wedding. Charlie, James, and Mrs. Charlie drove up from New Town for the occasion. Pirate brought them in the cart, and they met the Reverend and Mrs. McPherson and Maria along the way. Maria looked especially lovely in a blue dress with her blond hair pinned up in braids around her head.

"You look like a grown lady," James gasped, when he recognized the attractive young woman.

"Thank you," Maria replied, blushing, embarrassed by the compliment.

Upon their arrival at the church, they found it almost full with members of the regular congregation and many guests. Old Cyrus looked amazingly clean, dressed in good clothes. He had left his pipe at home, and Robert, also dressed in new clothes, accompanied him into the church. It was not a place where Old Cyrus felt comfortable, and he tripped as he entered the right side pew reserved for the groom's family. Charlie followed Cyrus and sat behind him with Mrs. Charlie, Mrs. Glynis and Miss Gwynn. Dr. Hughes' widow sat in the pew with Mrs. Glynis, Ellen, and Annie.

Carrie and her boys found places in the gallery, which delighted Tommy because he could see everyone come in and he and Zack were not blinded by the ladies' spring hats.

The music started, and Herr Becker brought Pine Blossom down the aisle toward a fashionably dressed Spotted Deer, who stood ashen-faced beside Robert in front of the altar.

Pine Blossom's two sisters were her bridesmaids, and her father walked her down the aisle. She looked radiant in her white dress, with her dark hair braided and pinned up around her head. Frau Becker had cleverly worked the Indian beads into a pattern around the neckline of the wedding dress. The effect was beautiful and signified her Shawnee background.

Spotted Deer stared at the radiant young girl before him. Was this the Pine Blossom he knew? The Lutheran minister, Reverend Fischer, smiled at the wedding party. Reverend McPherson stood to one side as they welcomed the bride, her father, and her two bridesmaids.

Spotted Deer came forward, with Robert as his best man. The lad looked handsome in his new clothes and with his new haircut. His hands shook as he held them in front of him. Robert whispered encouragement to the frightened groom.

The congregation stood up, and the service began. Herr Becker said his part in German, and then gave Pine Blossom's hand to Spotted Deer. Robert presented Reverend Fischer with the plain wedding band, and then sat down in the first pew. Reverend McPherson asked Spotted Deer the necessary questions in English, and the ceremony continued in German.

Old Cyrus watched the ceremony with tears running down his cheeks. The loss of his Rachel seemed especially keen that morning. Charlie leaned forward from the pew behind and offered Cyrus his handkerchief.

Cyrus accepted it in silence and wiped his tears. He felt sure that, outside, a lone hawk circled the church. Rachel's messenger would come to share this most poignant ceremony. Spotted Deer's wedding marked the end of his apprenticeship with Cyrus, and from now on, their relationship would be different. Old Cyrus would miss the lad. Spotted Deer would still come to help on the farm, but it would not be the same. Although he was glad for the boy, Cyrus couldn't help but feel sad and lonely.

Charlie and Sally rejoiced in Spotted Deer's good fortune. Pine Blossom was a lovely young woman and a most suitable bride for the Shawnee lad.

Robert found the ceremony beautiful and felt that the lives of these young people were full of promise. It seemed appropriate for Spotted Deer to move on and to live his own life, and the couple symbolized for Robert the hope and future of America. He experienced a strange mixture of emotions. Though he felt old and redundant, he also felt happy for the glowing bride and nervous groom, and he was honored to be part of their special day.

Outside, white clouds built and rebuilt, and the sun shone on a peaceful Shenandoah Valley. Pirate nickered, impatient to go home. A donkey brayed in an adjacent field, and a cow mooed in reply.

In the church, Spotted Deer placed the ring on Pine Blossom's finger, and the organ wheezed a little as the bellows filled with air. The bride and groom turned from the altar and recessed down the aisle toward the front door.

Old Cyrus wiped his eyes and blew his nose on Charlie's handkerchief. It was a new beginning and a sad ending. He sat down again and waited until his feet grew more able to carry him to the front door.

"Come, Cyrus," Robert said to the old man. "It's all over now."

"Not yet," Cyrus replied. "Not yet. Spotted Deer was like my son, and I loved him. He's gone now."

Robert led Old Cyrus toward the front door. The bright May morning greeted them. Outside a pair of red-tailed hawks circled above the church, their wings brilliant in the sunlight.

"I knew they would come," Cyrus remarked, and he shaded his eyes to see them. "I am not alone anymore. Rachel sent them to me to let me know I'm not alone.

## FICKLEVILLE

After Spotted Deer's wedding, he and Pine Blossom moved into Winchester. He still farmed for Robert, and Pine Blossom helped Blodwen on Yorweth's farm several days a week. Robert found he had less time to go fishing, and he remained busy with his farm.

Old Cyrus knew a great deal about caring for animals, and he helped Robert with the cows and the sheep. When Robert felt lonely, he rode Light Horse Harry to visit Yorweth and Blodwen on Sunday afternoons. Sometimes Mrs. Glynis and Miss Gwynn would also come to visit the couple, so Robert began to see the bright, cheerful Welsh ladies at his neighbors' house.

Annie and Ellen liked to ride out to see Blodwen, and these visits soon gave their father a social life. Meanwhile, Old Cyrus enlarged the cabin and added an additional room.

"Your cabin feels more like a real home," Annie remarked one Sunday afternoon as she sat in her father's enlarged house. "Why do you keep building on to it?"

"I'm not sure what I want," Robert said. "I'm trying to make the cabin bigger and more comfortable for you and Ellen. I am not interested in architecture, just comfort and convenience."

"You have a main room and three bedrooms. The loft is used for storage, there is an alcove for the two dogs, and you have a central fireplace. And now you plan another bedroom?" Annie asked her father. "You can't decide upon what you want. I'll call this house 'Fickleville.'"

Robert laughed. "That's a good name. 'Fickleville' it is, then."

"Papa, how do you plan to manage now that Spotted Deer is married?" Ellen asked.

"I have Spotted Deer several days a week, and with Old Cyrus and the builders that Will Holliday sent out, we're doing all right. I was hoping you and Annie would help when you're free on weekends and in the summer. I want to make this house less rustic and more comfortable for women," Robert replied.

He looked around the enlarged cabin and realized it had few feminine touches. "I wish Mrs. Glynis would come to visit," he continued. "But she's busy with her school teaching. She's good company and a great cook. I also can talk of Wales with her."

"I'm sure she'd come if you'd ask her on a weekend," Annie said. "I see her every day, and she usually inquires after you."

"I don't like to bother her if she's busy, but I do enjoy her company. I'll see her on my next visit at Yorweth's farm. That's a shorter trip for her, and I hate to ask her to come this far." Robert offered his daughters some of Old Cyrus' homemade locust pod beer. "It's good and not too strong," he assured them.

"Why don't you ask Mrs. Glynis to come for a visit this next weekend?" Ellen suggested. "She's quite concerned about how you're getting on without Spotted Deer's full-time help."

Robert sat down in an easy chair Blodwen had given to him. Blodwen had also brought him a low footstool, which she had covered with wool woven from her own sheep. She made it into a Red Dragon pattern reminiscent of Wales.

Robert put more coal on the fire because the evening felt damp and chilly. Annie heated a pot of stew she'd made to share with her sister and father. Ellen sliced a loaf of Carrie's good bread and spread fresh butter on the slices.

They ate a simple supper and drank more of Old Cyrus' locust pod beer. Monty and Danny joined them as the twilight gathered over the mountains. Old Cyrus entered the cabin after he finished the evening chores.

"Good evening to you, Miss Ellen and Miss Annie," Cyrus greeted the family. "I hope you left some beer for me. That stew smells mighty good."

"We saved you some," Annie told him. "Papa says you have all kinds of beer stored in the loft."

"Hit won't be there for long if we give hit to everyone who drops in." Old Cyrus found his rocking chair and sat down. "That pillow you made for me, Annie, sure helps my back. I'd swap a gallon of beer for a few more creature comforts."

"Here's your stew, Cyrus," Annie said, offering him a bowl.

"Hit sure does smell grand. Just like a bandquet. You're almost as good a cook as Carrie." Cyrus ate the beef stew with great pleasure. It was filled with home-grown potatoes and carrots. He drank a long swallow of beer. "Yes, in fact, you're almost as good a cook as Mrs. Glynis," Cyrus said, wondering if Robert understood his remark in its full meaning. "Yes, ma'am, you girls are turning into real capable Shenandoah Valley women." He gave a piece of stew meat to Danny, who growled at Monty to stay away from his treat.

"Here's your bit," Robert said, giving Monty his own piece. "Cyrus, you're spoiling these dogs."

"I know, but I love it, and so do the dogs. A little spoiling never hurt anyone." Cyrus rocked in his chair and continued eating his stew.

"Ask Mrs. Glynis to come out soon, Papa," Annie demanded. "It's good for us to have company and visit with our neighbors."

Robert seemed lost in thought and did not respond. He simply looked at his stew, as if searching for some answer in it.

"Robert!" said Old Cyrus, loudly, putting his stew bowl down on the table and helping himself to some more locust pod beer. "Robert, you need a philosophy."

"What do you mean, a philosophy?" Robert asked. "What kind of talk is that?"

"You don't understand the wild creatures and their meaning. You have no faith in the great birds that fly over this valley," Cyrus said, struggling to express his thoughts. "I get messages from my wife, Rachel, through the hawks and from the great eagles, which nest here or use the mountains as a passageway to other places."

Cyrus still couldn't find the right words to make Robert understand, but he continued. "Robert, you got to learn some philosophy. That's what made Mr. Jefferson such a good leader. He had a philosophy that young men need education. It had a few high-toned French ideas that don't scow here, but his philosophy was a good one."

"I don't know anything about Mr. Jefferson," Robert said. "I'm lost in a strange country without my wife."

"That's just it, Robert. You need to study the birds, those marvelous golden eagles that live in our mountains."

## ROBERT'S FUTURE

The following Sunday was a clear day, with cloudless skies and a light breeze across the mountains that kept the sun from becoming too hot. That morning, Mrs. Glynis and Miss Gwynn rode out to see Robert and his girls. Dr. Mason kindly lent his team of black horses, and Golden Eagle drove the Welsh ladies from Winchester to Robert's farm.

"I hope Mrs. Glynis likes your new room," Annie remarked as she saw the team and carriage on the ridge. "It's hardly finished, and yet it really adds to the space at Fickleville."

"I'll get the table set for the tea," Ellen offered. "I made some scones in the new brick oven. It looks like it will be quite a festive party." She laid the table and put the kettle on the fire for tea.

Hoping for a snack, Monty lay under Robert's chair and followed him with watchful eyes. Danny and Old Cyrus remained at the barn to look after the horses.

Mrs. Glynis and Miss Gwynn arrived around midday. Cyrus climbed up on the ridge to meet them and led Marcus and Lafayette down to the barn.

"What a lovely afternoon!" Mrs. Glynis exclaimed as she stepped out of the carriage with Cyrus' help.

"Yes, ma'am, it's a perfect day," Old Cyrus agreed.

He helped Miss Gwynn down and saw Robert walk up from the cabin on the path beside the stream.

Robert smiled as he greeted his guests. "It's good to see you! You picked a lovely day for a visit." He helped the ladies with their oak baskets.

"We've brought you and Old Cyrus a ham for lunch," said Mrs. Glynis. "Will Holliday brought it to us and said Charlie sent it up by stagecoach." She lifted the ham in its basket from the carriage.

"We'll enjoy that," said Robert as he took the heavy

basket. "Miss Gwynn, how is your school progressing?"

"We have twenty children now, and more coming," she replied. "Winchester is growing, and we've added another classroom to the present building to keep up with the demand."

Old Cyrus led the horses into the upper barn, where he and Golden Eagle unhooked them from their carriage. Then they led Marcus and Lafayette into stalls in the lower part of the barn.

The stream, fed by the snow melting in the mountains, babbled over rocks as the water came down the valley. The new leaves made a crazy-quilt pattern of various shades of green, with the stately pines standing like sentinels among the lighter green foliage.

"Come," said Robert. "I want to show you Fickleville, as Annie calls my house."

"Fickleville?" repeated Miss Gwynn. "When did you start calling your cabin that?"

"Annie says I can't make up my mind, and we keep making additions to it. She's right, of course. We're just adding a new bedroom. It's not quite finished, but it will make the house bigger." Robert explained. "Come, ladies, we'll take the path beside the stream." He led them down from the barn through a fairyland of green leaves, dogwood blossoms, and wildflowers toward the cabin.

Suddenly, a large bird flew above them and alighted beside the stream on the branch of a chestnut tree. Here, he gazed down at the four people below him.

"Look," pointed Old Cyrus excitedly. "That's a golden eagle. He's one of the most beautiful birds in the valley."

The walkers stopped and looked at the eagle above them. The noble creature gazed down at Robert's farm as if all the world belonged to him.

"He's the king of birds. The poets write about the golden eagle," said Old Cyrus. He looked up in wonder at the great bird of prey perched on the tree limb.

"How do you know about poetry?" Miss Gwynn asked Cyrus. "You hardly know how to read and write."

"There was a wise man in the North Carolina mountains who knew how to do both, and he carried a book of poems with him. He read them aloud to us children on the porch on summer evenings until it grew too dark to see. George Umstead was his name. A fine old gent he was, too. He wore a tall silk hat, and always told the grandest tales and recited the most adventuresome poems. I'm only half-educated, Miss Gwynn, but I remember what I hear, even if I did come from the mountains. We've got some educated folks there, too."

Old Cyrus felt cross at her remarks about his meager education. He was proud of his storytelling friend. Old Cyrus took pride in being able to read a little. Now, with Zack's help once a week, he could read even more.

"The eagles don't like crowded places," Cyrus continued. "They like solitude away from people. I'll go put the lambs in the barn so Mr. Eagle here won't decide they'd make a good dinner."

Old Cyrus walked back to the barn with Monty and Danny to herd the young lambs into stalls and let Harry and Daniel Morgan out into the pasture. "The eagle won't bother horses," he said aloud, as he walked away.

"Oh, I think I've upset Cyrus," said Miss Gwynn. She was a kind lady, and she hated hurting anyone's feelings.

"You were rather sharp with him," admitted Mrs. Glynis, as they continued down the path.

"Yes, you're right," said Miss Gwynn. "What a rude thing to say! I don't know what got into me. Perhaps I'd better apologize. I'll go talk to him, and he can show me back to the cabin," she said. She hurried after Old Cyrus, who was striding toward the barn in a huff.

"Oh, dear, I hope he's all right," Mrs. Glynis said.

"Old Cyrus? He'll be just fine. He doesn't hold grudges. He'll have forgotten any insult by dinner time," Robert assured her.

In the midst of this conversation, Mrs. Glynis and Robert forgot about the golden eagle. Now, they looked above their heads and found the bird was still there, unruffled by the visitors. Robert and Mrs. Glynis stood transfixed and watched the eagle until it finally raised its wings, lifted itself onto the air currents, and flew westward.

Robert followed the great bird's passage across the valley, struck by its nobility and courage. Here was a bird that lived a solitary life in the wilderness. Robert realized that he, like the eagle, must also make a meaningful life. He had been living in his Welsh past, and now it was the time to be connected to something in America's present.

"What a marvelous bird," he said, turning toward Mrs. Glynis. "He lives in the mountains and seeks the loneliest places."

"He's beautiful," whispered Mrs. Glynis. "He's the grandest bird I've seen in America. He seems to tell us to go forward and make a new life."

"Yes," agreed Robert. "A new life. A life away from the coalfields of Wales. A life of firsts and new beginnings in a new land. Sarah never understood that."

They remained on the path. Robert looked out over the valley beyond them. He saw the lambs in the field and Cyrus talking with Miss Gwynn. He couldn't be sure, but he thought they were again friends.

Mrs. Glynis finally spoke, breaking their silence. "Birds can live a lonely life, but people need each other, Mr. Jones. We are not solitary creatures."

"Yes, I realize that now," Robert said. "I've neglected my girls. They come to see me, but they don't stay. It's too quiet for them."

"No—your cabin is not a woman's home. It's a bachelor's house," replied Mrs. Glynis.

"I've been blind," Robert confessed. "I've been locked in my own grief. I believe that golden eagle came in all of its majesty and opened my eyes." He paused, collecting his thoughts.

"It's lonely out here, miles from town," said Mrs. Glynis. "But you have cows and sheep and new spring lambs. This farm, with the help of Old Cyrus and Spotted Deer, is successful. And you don't have to remain all alone, Mr. Jones. What do you wish for your future?"

Mrs. Glynis and Robert walked slowly toward the cabin. Suddenly, Robert stopped and looked at the pretty Welsh woman by his side. Her intelligent face was lifted toward his as her dark eyes searched the sky for the eagle.

"He's gone," she said at last. "That beautiful creature is on the other side of the Allegheny mountains."

In that moment, Robert realized that Mrs. Glynis would make his life complete. He blushed and felt shy, yet he knew he must speak now or he might not find the courage again.

"Mrs. Glynis, uh, I don't know your given name," he stammered, as he stopped on the path.

"My name is Elizabeth."

"May I call you that? I wish you would call me by my name, Robert."

"I would like that, Robert. And, yes, you may call me Elizabeth."

Robert took a steadying breath. "Elizabeth, would you share your life with me? I'm expanding the cabin again. I've sold some beautiful sheep pelts, and the wool business is successful. You could keep teaching, but I need you." He stopped and looked at her, unsure of her reply. "I know I don't have much—only this farm and a funny added-onto house."

"Yes, but that's enough, Robert, and we'd do well together," Elizabeth answered. "We'll have to wait a while, I suppose, to fill out the year since Sarah died."

Robert experienced a strange mixture of emotions. He felt overwhelmed by happiness and relief at her answer, but he wanted to respect Sarah. "I'm not sure what would be appropriate," he confessed. "I'll ask the rector at Christ Church in Winchester. Still, I'd rather not wait. We could get married quietly, just us, Gwynn, and the two girls."

Robert clasped Elizabeth's hand. A new life in this new country stretched before them, filled with hope. The golden eagle, that lover of solitude, had flown away.

# BIBLIOGRAPHY

American Heritage. *The American Heritage Book of the Presidents and Famous Americans.* New York: Dell, 1967.

Brown, Katharine L., Nancy T. Sorrells, and Kenneth E. Koons. *Virginia's Cattle Story: The First Four Centuries.* Staunton, VA: Lot's Wife, 2004.

Buchanan, John. *The Road to Guilford Courthouse: The American Revolution in the Carolinas.* John Wiley & Sons, 1997.

Casey, Betty. *The Complete Book of Square Dancing.* Garden City, NY: Doubleday, 1976.

Kephart, Horace, Harold F. Farwell, and J. Karl Nicholas. *Smoky Mountain Voices: A Lexicon of Southern Appalachian Speech Based on the Research of Horace Kephart.* Lexington: University of Kentucky Press, 1993.

Mayo, Margot. *The American Square Dance.* New York: Sentinel, 1948.

McDowell, Flora L., *Folk Dances of Tennessee: Folk Customs and Old Play Party Games of the Caney Fork Valley.* Delaware, Ohio: Cooperative Recreation Services, Inc. Date unknown.

Parry-Jones, D. *Welsh Legends & Fairy Lore.* Marboro Books, 1992.

Pancake, John S. *This Destructive War: The British Campaign in the Carolinas, 1780-1782.* Birmingham: University of Alabama Press, 1985.

Rankin, Hugh F. *Francis Marion: The Swamp Fox*. New York: Crowell, 1973.

Rouse, Parke. *The Great Wagon Road: From Philadelphia to the South*. New York: McGraw-Hill, 1973.

Russell, David Lee. *The American Revolution in the Southern Colonies*. Jefferson, NC: McFarland, 2000.

Smith, Andrew F. *The Oxford Encyclopedia of Food and Drink in America*. Oxford University Press, 2004.

Sobel, Dava. *Longitude: The True Story of a Lone Genius Who Solved the Greatest Scientific Problem of His Time*. New York: Walker, 1995.

Southern, Ed. *Voices of the American Revolution in the Carolinas*. Winston-Salem, NC: John F. Blair, 2009.

Strunk, William, and E. B. White, *The Elements of Style*. New York: Macmillan, 1979.

Suter, Scott Hamilton. *Shenandoah Valley Folklife*. Jackson, MS: University of Mississippi Press, 1999.

Wilder, Roy. *You All Spoken Here: A Handy Illustrate Guide to Carryin' on in the South...*Raleigh, NC: Gourd Hollow, 1975.

# ACKNOWLEDGMENTS

I gratefully acknowledge the generous help offered to me by these people and institutions:

- Davis Library and Wilson Library at the University of North Carolina in Chapel Hill, especially Wilson's Southern Historical Collection.
- Diane Steinhaus at the Music Library of the University of North Carolina in Chapel Hill.
- Robert Butler and Michael Kelleher at Bray Library, County Wicklow, Ireland.
- Ryan Walker, from The American Livestock Breeds Conservancy in Pittsboro, NC.
- Keith A. Brintzenhoff, for his help with square-dance calls and the German, Pennsylvania Dutch, and Scots-Irish influences in the Shenandoah Valley.
- Burwell Ware, for the spelling of "Rambeau."
- Alisa Huff, for visiting Winchester to find information.
- Ingrid and Peter McIlwain from Enniskerry, Ireland, for information about the bodhrán.
- Dr. James Pruett and Mrs. Lillian Pruett, who provided additional musical information.
- My sister, Holly Pulsifer, who provided information about wagons and carriages and found books on women who traveled west, often against their will and under difficult conditions.
- Colin Dickson, for his help with the description of historic Philadelphia and the Great Valley Road.
- Eugene Alston, for information about honey locust pod beer, moonshine whiskey, literacy, uncontrollable pigs, and street lighting in Winchester, VA, in 1828.
- The Historical Museum of Winchester in Winchester, VA.
- The Museum of the Shenandoah Valley in Winchester, VA.
- Richard and Cynthia Fox, who owned a Wild Bird Center and helped with information about birds.

- Rick Heeren and Bruce Ladd, also of the Wild Bird Center, who provided additional information.
- David Ballantyne, who helped me with information about the German Palatines, Moselle/Mosel River wines, English expressions and grammar, and whether the Highland Regiment could be pulled down in a swift river by their woolen kilts.
- Joe Mitchem at Davis Library for help with the Battle of Kings Mountain and how the Tarheels got their name.
- Conrad and Alice Perry, for information about Pennsylvania's flora and fauna, the history of the Pennsylvania Dutch, and the settlements in Lancaster and York counties.
- Carline Simpson, a University of North Carolina graduate student at Chapel Hill, for her information on pretzels and the vendors in Philadelphia.
- Tyler Gilmore, a University of North Carolina student at Chapel Hill, for his help in history.
- Timothy Richardson, Claudia Dayson, and Luba Sawczyn, of the Chapel Hill Library, for their help in getting books for me on various subjects and for answering difficult and obscure questions.
- Righter Publishing Company (Timberlake, NC), which has published four of my books.
- Rachel Kiel, who has been invaluable with her help doing endless corrections and making many printouts of the manuscript.
- Meghan Lubker, who supplied the pictures of the Shenandoah Valley's houses and barns.
- Susan Kent, for her thorough reading of the manuscript.
- My editors, Rita Berman, Peggy Ellis, and Alice Perry, for their peerless editorial assistance, encouragement, and support.
- Lance Haworth, for his editing and help with understanding the topography of Wales.

- Eugene Alston—again—for his patience.

Many thanks also to those other friends and acquaintances who have been helpful, and thank you all for seeing this story to its conclusion.

—Ariana Mangum

Other Books by Ariana Mangum

*Carlos, the Mouse Who Discovered America*

*A Forgotten Landscape*

*When the Goldenrod Sang in the Meadows*

*Where the Butterflies Roam*

\*\*\*

Enjoy Other Fine Books from Righter Publishing Company

Thrillers, detective stories, short story collections, children's books, inspirational works, poetry collections, family histories, science fiction, romance, literary fiction, local histories, personal memoirs and self-help.

Go to www.righterbooks.com

www.ingramcontent.com/pod-product-compliance
Lightning Source LLC
Chambersburg PA
CBHW071114160426
43196CB00013B/2568